# THE BOOK BUSINESS

## WHAT EVERYONE NEEDS TO KNOW®

# THE BOOK BUSINESS

## WHAT EVERYONE NEEDS TO KNOW®

### MIKE SHATZKIN AND ROBERT PARIS RIGER

# OXFORD
UNIVERSITY PRESS

Oxford University Press is a department of the University of Oxford. It furthers the University's objective of excellence in research, scholarship, and education by publishing worldwide. Oxford is a registered trademark of Oxford University Press in the UK and certain other countries.

"What Everyone Needs to Know" is a registered trademark of Oxford University Press.

Published in the United States of America by Oxford University Press 198 Madison Avenue, New York, NY 10016, United States of America.

Library of Congress Cataloging-in-Publication Data
Names: Shatzkin, Mike, author. | Riger, Robert Paris., author.
Title: The book business : what everyone needs to know /
Mike Shatzkin and Robert Paris Riger.
Description: New York, NY : Oxford University Press, [2019] | Series: What everyone needs to know | Includes bibliographical references and index.
Identifiers: LCCN 2018030696 (print) | LCCN 2018033488 (ebook) |
ISBN 9780190628055 (updf) | ISBN 9780190628062 (epub) |
ISBN 9780190628048 (pbk. : alk. paper) |
ISBN 9780190628031 (cloth : alk. paper)
Subjects: LCSH: Publishers and publishing—United States. |
Booksellers and bookselling—United States. |
Book industries and trade—United States.
Classification: LCC Z471 (ebook) | LCC Z471.S4425 2019 (print) |
DDC 070.50973—dc23
LC record available at https://lccn.loc.gov/2018030696

1 3 5 7 9 8 6 4 2

Paperback printed by Sheridan Books, Inc., United States of America
Hardback printed by Bridgeport National Bindery, Inc., United States of America

# CONTENTS

| | |
|---|---|
| FOREWORD | vii |
| ACKNOWLEDGMENTS | xiii |
| 1 The Global Book Business | 1 |
| 2 From Idea to Book | 12 |
| 3 Bookselling, Marketing, and Sales: Getting the Book to the Reader | 31 |
| 4 Some Publishing History | 49 |
| 5 E-Books | 57 |
| 6 The Book Publishing Business Model | 70 |
| 7 Bookselling in the Twenty-First Century— Amazon.com | 81 |

8   Children's and Young Adult (YA) Publishing          106

9   Audiobooks                                          113

10  The Future of Publishing                            122

GLOSSARY                                                145
INDEX                                                   157

# FOREWORD

Book Production (Publishing) is not the mysterious rite which many people seem to think it is. Almost everyone knows a publisher, or someone in a publishing office, or an author or an author's friend, yet it is surprising how little people know about the publishing business and how many odd things they imagine.

Stanley M. Rinehart
President of the AAP and Farrar & Rinehart
*New York Times*, 1936

### Why should you read this book?

*The Book Business: What Everyone Needs to Know®* is an insider's guide to trade book publishing in the United States: the book that can help you if you are thinking of writing a book, looking for a career in publishing, thinking of investing in the publishing business, or if you're just an avid reader who wants to know how books travel from a writer's mind to a reader's hands. This production cycle from manuscript to publication has always been mysterious to those outside the industry—it appears as a veritable black box. The making of a book seems to take longer and to require the talents of more diverse people than anyone outside the process can imagine. Perhaps surprisingly, it is also often the case that people in large publishing houses, and also some important players who operate outside the publishing house, only really understand their specific role, or their department's role, in the publishing process.

This book is focused on "trade" or "consumer" book publishing, largely books that sell through brick-and-mortar stores and through the online digital booksellers. (Bookstores, libraries, and the wholesalers that serve them are "the book trade.") We explore various subareas of trade publishing in the United States, each of which has its own history and expectations: hardcover, mass-market paperback, trade paperback, children's, audio, and digital.

We remember a telling story from the early '90s of the number-one literary agent—a man who had built his business on the front end of the deal, enticing publishers with great new authors and works, who was a master of the art of the auction, the preempt, and all of the behind-the-scenes intel that a literary *macher* could manipulate to maximize the advance. (Reader: if you do not know exactly what an advance is yet, we will get there.) Despite his expert knowledge of the agent-author-publisher relationship, he found himself one day needing to know more about the publisher one of his clients had just signed with. To get the most from the deal and to ensure this author's future at the publishing house, the agent had to learn about the publisher up close. To do so, he hired a publishing consulting firm (as the reader may have guessed, a firm at which one of the authors was the principal consultant) to walk him through some of the more arcane workings of book publishing. What qualified as arcane to this prominent agent, with years of publishing experience? The ordinary goings-on within the publishing house. This may be surprising, but it's not unusual. The players in and around trade book publishing can be very narrow in their knowledge about the industry and still be very good at their jobs. It's no wonder that to those outside the industry, the picture is even blurrier. And with the rate of change in publishing accelerating, it is more of a mystery even to the biggest bibliophiles among us.

The authors of this book have between them well over eight decades of experience in the book business. Robert has been on the senior staff of several of the industry's largest companies; the consulting experiences of both Robert and Mike touch virtually every important player in the English-language publishing world over the past half-century. And they have had significant exposure to many of the non-English players as well. They come to writing this book with thorough knowledge of "how it is done" by the pros. Despite this, both Robert and Mike are unconventional thinkers and have challenged many of the industry's standard practices throughout their careers. In this book, their primary job is to describe how publishing works and why. Over the course of the book, they also challenge many of the most conventional practices in the business.

This book was written during a long era of great change in book publishing. As the cliché goes, the internet changed everything, and more than two decades after it arrived, it hasn't finished changing things yet. The movement of sales from brick-and-mortar stores to online retailers, which overwhelmingly means Amazon, and the new reality that consumers find out about books largely through online channels have required publishers to adjust all their thinking about how they put books into the marketplace. The development of digital delivery of books (e-books) has also changed things, but the biggest impacts have been on how printed books find their readers.

Publishers before never had a single customer who accounted for half or more of their sales, a position that Amazon now holds for many. The size of a publisher's sales force has become less important. The digital marketing capabilities of a publisher are not as obvious as a big sales force, but they've become increasingly critical. Publishers used to routinely ignore publicity breaks on older books because, without copies in the stores, sales wouldn't result from amplifying those breaks. That's no longer true. (Rest assured that if some of these terms are new to you, they will be explained over the course of the book. Defining the main terms and concepts is a major part of the book's purpose.)

Not only is book publishing living in a different world from the one it was in five or ten or twenty years ago; it is not clear to anybody exactly what the publishing ecosystem will look like five or ten or twenty years from now. Online sales today represent more than half of all sales for most publishers, and they're still growing. How far will that go? As of this writing, Barnes & Noble is closing stores, Amazon is opening them, and independent stores are enjoying a renaissance, but nobody is predicting with any certainty how long those trends will continue or whether they will accelerate. Self-publishing is no longer growing explosively, but the potential remains for a "United Artists" attempt, whereby branded authors might band together to create their own publishing house. Amazon Publishing pulled back from going after broad-based bestsellers in favor of working in genres, but as their share and new brick-and-mortar presence grow, might they try again to go after big books?

Publishing has always been a bit mysterious because it is so complicated. Mike has long said that "publishing any book presents the opportunity to make an infinite number of decisions, which, for the sake of commercial viability and sanity, must be resisted." Big publishers standardize as much as they can but still, as the reader of this book will see, there are many steps—from a title's being acquired (usually before it is completely written) to its delivery to its ultimate reader. Mike and Robert spell all that out and demystify the publishing process.

But they won't make it simple, because publishing isn't simple. And they won't make clear what will happen in the years to come because, near as they can tell, nobody knows. But they will point you in the right direction.

### A Note from Mike Shatzkin

A sad note that is important to readers: about three weeks after Robert and I turned in the "final version" of our manuscript, he passed away suddenly and unexpectedly. This meant that I had to finish the job, including responding to the reader reviews provided by our publisher. There is no substitute for Robert's insight and imagination, even though we had friends who could help me with segments of the business he knew a lot better than I: audio and kids' books being most prominent among them. As a personal matter, it is just so terribly sad that my gifted and warmhearted friend couldn't share in the really *fun* part of being an author: talking about your book to promote it and seeing the observations of smart people who read it and take the time to comment on it.

# ACKNOWLEDGMENTS

Sanj Kharbanda, former executive, Houghton Mifflin, now Beacon Press; Betsy Groban, head of Kids Publishing, Houghton Mifflin; Jeffrey Capshew, vice president, sales, Macmillan; Alison Lazarus, then president, sales division, Macmillan, now at Hachette; Sally Richardson, president and publisher, St. Martin's Press; Barbara Marcus, president and publisher, Children's Random House; Lorraine Shanley, founder, Market Partners International; Michael Cader, creator of Publishers Lunch and Publisher's Marketplace; Amy Berkower, chairman, Writer's House Literary Agency; Peggy Intrator, consultant, Scholastic; Susan Weinberg, senior vice president and group publisher, Perseus Book Group; Judith Curr, president, formerly publisher, and founder of Atria Books, now at HarperCollins; Andrea Fleck-Nesbit, executive director of business operations, Workman Publishing; Brian DeFiore, founder of Defiore and Co., Literary Agency; Daniel Weiss, children's publishing guru; Tom McCormick, former president of St. Martin's Press; Sarah Lieberman, vice president, audio, Simon & Schuster; Roz Parr, marketing director, Alfred A. Knopf; Max Rudin, Library of America; Brian McCarthy, Library of America; Constance Sayre, co-founder, Market Partners International; John Ingram, chairman of Ingram

Content Group; the pseudonymous Data Guy, an industry data analyst; Scott MacIntyre, formerly Douglas & McIntyre, Canada; Audio Publishers Association (APB); Association of American (AAP).

# THE BOOK BUSINESS

## WHAT EVERYONE NEEDS TO KNOW®

# 1

# THE GLOBAL BOOK BUSINESS

### What are the various segments within the book business and how do they differ?

The "book business" referred to in the title of this book is largely the trade book business in the United States. It seemed worth putting this segment of the overall global book publishing market in context. Accurately sizing the existing global market for books and attributing reasonable numbers for each component of the industry by country is as hard as solving a Rubik's cube when one or more squares are missing.

### What are the key segments of the global book publishing industry?

Trade
Religious
Higher Education
El-Hi—Elementary and High School
Professional/Technical

### What is trade book publishing?

The most visible segment of publishing—the one most people think of when they think of "book publishing"—is trade publishing. It gets its name because its primary avenue of distribution is the "book trade," defined as bookstores and libraries and the wholesalers that serve them. It is the most visible and influential segment of the book business but not the largest by volume

Over the past two decades, online retail has gone from almost nonexistent to a very substantial subcategory of its own. It has other players and components, but it basically consists of Amazon.

### What are the components of trade publishing?

Trade is hardly a unified business; it is seen by its practitioners as comprising a number of segments, some tightly integrated, that are identified by a book's format:

Hardcover—Fiction, Nonfiction, and Reference
Trade Paperback
Mass-Market Paperback
E-Book or Digital Publishing
Audiobook Publishing—Digital Download and CDs
Children's Publishing
Picture Book
Paperback
Chapter Book
Novelty

### Is mass-market publishing still distinct from trade publishing?

Mass-market publishing is now pretty much integrated with trade publishing functionally, but it has distinct roots from the days when it operated in a channel walled off from trade books. Trade publishing placed its books in bookstores by negotiated distribution that required each store to individually order each copy of every title, the theory being that the booksellers knew their audience best and were the ultimate arbiter of what books were chosen to line the store's shelves. Putting that power in the booksellers' hands actually generated a substantial expense of doing business because it created the need for negotiations at the outset and for a buyer to make decisions for every order and reorder.

After World War II, a new breed of publisher put standardized rack-sized paperback books (often called "pocket books" as a generic term, borrowing the brand name of the first US company in the business) in front of consumers through the wholesalers that placed magazines on newsstands and in certain mass merchandise outlets. For about two decades, those publishers were distinct. But as their distribution moved into bookstores and the magazine wholesaler distribution choked on the title volume it was being asked to handle, producing large returns, mass-market paperbacks integrated into the trade business.

A number of factors drove the integration of mass-market with trade publishing. The high value of mass-market rights was reflected in the advances paid to hardcover publishers for mass-market rights. But then the hardcover publishers got only half of the royalties (dividing these with the author) rather than a full profit. Over time, the biggest mass-market outlets—like drugstore chains—started buying directly from the publishers rather than through the mass-market wholesalers. This weakened the unique mass segment—the independent distributors, known in the business as ID wholesalers, who were the wholesalers of magazines and paperbacks that comprised the original mass-market distribution system—and created a sales profile that trade publishers could handle. Over time, the mass and trade houses combined, and the biggest books got "hard-soft" deals instead of auctioned paperback rights. Today all the companies that publish for the mass-market channel also publish trade books, and most of the mass-market books sold today are sold through trade channels. Because trade publishing is so broad in what it includes (any conceivable topic), audiences (across all ages and levels of seriousness), and formats (hardcovers, paperbacks, e-books, audiobooks), there are subsets of trade that become specialties for some publishers. There are publishers that do only genre fiction and others that do only books for juvenile readers. That specialization creates differentiation in the capabilities and practices of the publishers.

### How do the sales and distribution strategies of college and elementary and high school publishing differ from consumer or trade publishers?

College textbook publishers and el-hi (elementary and high school) textbook publishers depend on professors and teachers and school systems to decide to purchase and use their books. Their sales operations are quite different from those of trade publishers, and the books often reach their customers without passing through any trade accounts.

The trade is virtually irrelevant to them. They have to do their marketing to very specific and targeted audiences, and the sales function is almost always working with institutions that purchase for groups of individual users, totally unlike what consumer publishers do.

### How do academic and university presses operate within the trade environment?

Academic and professional publishers use bookstores as secondary channels of distribution. They primarily talk to their audiences more directly. Professional publishing—sometimes called "STEM" for "scientific, technical, educational, and medical," but which also includes books aimed at lawyers and accountants—moves a lot of its books by direct marketing to its audience and through conventions and conferences where their audiences gather and can be easily targeted.

University press publishers, a subset of academic publishers with close ties to specific universities, straddle trade and professional practices, with some presses being more dependent on a highly academic audience not reached through bookstores and others publishing many books that are primarily sold through bookstores. The biggest university press publishers—and Oxford University Press, the publisher of this book, is by far the largest in the world—are complex organizations publishing in a range of formats (sometimes including subscription journals, not just books). They are generally more rigorous about the content of their books than commercial trade houses, putting most of their books (including this one) through a process called "peer review" by which the book's content is examined and vetted by qualified experts in the topic the book covers. Publishing through a university press conveys a level of review and scrutiny that is not part of the brand promise of a commercial trade publisher.

### What is religious publishing?

The books produced by religious book publishers are, like trade books, aimed at everyday people as end users, but in the case of religious titles their audience is devout readers in a variety of faiths. The largest subsegment is Bible publishing, which has an intricate set of rules on which editions are made for which group of buyers. We were once submitted an illustrated Bible by a book packager, and its depiction of Christ on the cross with stigmata rather than ropes meant that its market was limited, even if a stigmata errata sheet were added.

It is a market not to be entered lightly, without a deep understanding of the strong beliefs of its readers. As a result, religious publishing is highly insular, with little staff crossover and with a number of the key companies located in Nashville, Tennessee. These publishers also gather in their own conventions, sponsored by the Christian Booksellers Association, now known as the Association for Christian Retail, as their members also offer for sale Christian music, Christian merchandise—from crosses to elaborate garments worn while celebrating services—and Christian franchise opportunities.

### Why is this book focused primarily on trade publishing?

We focus on trade publishing because it is the branch of the industry that touches the most people and garners the most public attention. It is where the bestsellers come from. Sometimes referred to as "consumer book publishing," it is almost always the part of publishing people are talking about when publishing is discussed generally. If you are a passionate reader in your free time, the books you are reading are likely trade books, so this is the segment of publishing you will want to learn about. Likewise, if you have picked up this book because publishing as a career path calls to you, then likely it is visions of trade publishing, specifically, that fill your mind. Last, we believe trade publishing is inherently more complex than the other lines of book publishing and therefore requires a clear explanation.

### How is trade publishing organized?

In 1985, there were twelve key trade companies for whom we were able to get estimates of earnings. When we applied 2015 ownership to these twelve companies, the number shrank down to six companies that now controlled the volume encompassed by the twelve in our estimate in 1985. The top three companies in 1985 covered 48 percent of the trade business back then. If you apply the ownership matrix from 2015, the top three companies jump from covering 48 percent to 85 percent of the trade business today. This represents the much-talked-about trend of consolidation in publishing.

Now what had been the "Big Six" is the "Big Five" instead. In order of size, as of this writing, these are Penguin Random House, HarperCollins, Simon & Schuster, Hachette Book Group, and Macmillan. Within companies such as those in the Big Five are numerous imprints.

### What is an imprint?

Imprints are essentially mini-brands with their own specialties, focuses, identities, and often staffs. These are sometimes defined by genre. Some of these began as stand-alone publishing companies, so the proliferation of imprints connects to the larger trend toward consolidation.

From the perspective of publishers' trading partners downstream—bookstores, libraries, and wholesalers—imprints have real "identity." They are known by the books they publish and the ways they publish them. Customers will tend to generalize about their marketing capabilities and reliability, how good their editing or cover designs are, and, of course, the "character" of their lists. Knopf and Crown might both be "imprints" of Random House, but knowledgeable buyers will make and believe in real distinctions between them, as though they were separate companies.

Within a publisher, an imprint is, effectively, an "operating unit" working with shared central services. In most big publishers where we know the practices, the imprints are assigned notional profit-and-loss calculations that often affect the bonuses of the staff of those imprints. The head of the imprint, who could be an "editor-in-chief" or a "publisher," runs his or her own operation, which covers most of the single-title decisions about what to publish and how to publish it. Manufacturing, sales, and fulfillment are handled by central services. Publicity and title marketing live in the imprint. And rights sales tend to be centralized with the big house, although we have known of exceptions where the imprint kept that function.

Generally, small stuff is kept individualized within the imprint, and large stuff that depends on scale is handled by the owning house for all the imprints.

*How did the proliferation of imprints happen and what challenges does the structure create both for the imprint managements and for the big houses that own them?*

It has long been obvious to publishers that sales and warehousing benefited from increased size and scale but that editing and title marketing did not. It was natural for big publishers to want to add more volume "throughput" to support their scale operations. And it was just as natural for smaller publishers to see that their unit costs for everything were higher than the big guys' costs were. So the big houses could squeeze more margin out of every sale *and* make more sales. Acquisition and merger just followed logically.

Once combined, though, some rationalization—making rules so that the new imprints played nicely with the house's practices, policies, and other imprints—became necessary. Would a big house allow two imprints to "compete" in an auction for the same book? Obviously, rules were needed around that, and different houses make them differently. (Many, if not most, work out in advance which of their imprints will go after any particular title. But that's complicated too, because imprint heads have agent relationships, and many of them overlap.)

There are complications that arise on the rights and sales sides also. If you have a "customer" that wants books on knitting or books for troubled teenagers or books for dedicated sports fans, there is a good chance those books will exist in several different imprints in the house. Sometimes marketing opportunities require an "investment," and different imprint heads could have different ideas about what makes sense.

So the imprint structure was created for efficiency, but its existence creates efficiency challenges.

### Why have so many publishing companies been taken over by foreign ownership?

There has been an outcry over the majority of US book publishing companies having gradually fallen under the control of foreign companies, and the phenomenon is easy to track. In the thirty years covered by our data, the shift is from one company—under UK control accounting for between 5 and 10 percent of sales—to a landscape where 58 percent of sales are under foreign control. It is not clear *why* this shift to foreign ownership of US publishing has happened. But one possible reason is the change in the organization of the English-language world, which took place in the early 1970s. Before that time, the English-language world was divided by overt agreement between New York, where American publishers controlled the books in the United States and the Philippines, and London, where British publishers controlled the books throughout the rest of the English-language world, specifically Britain, Australia, India, South Africa, and the rest of the former "empire." The British publishers had sufficient power to enforce that division, effectively forcing American publishers and agents to sell their Commonwealth rights to a UK house for parceling out. Then the US publishers were forced by the Justice Department to stop this collusion in restraint of trade. US publishers signed a consent decree requiring them to open up the marketplace for future books. So they were no longer allowed to agree to the standard divisions that had always governed.

In effect, this converted the English language market from one that was about two equal pieces to one that was many pieces, with the United States being, by far, the single largest piece. That made US publishing attractive to own for many publishers, including all the British ones. And that might explain the fact that UK and German publishers own most of the industry in the United States today.

### What makes the book business different from all other businesses?

In a single word: "granularity." There are just so many *more* books than there are movies or TV shows or albums of music, and that effect alone would create massive differences in audience identification and marketing strategy. In figurative terms, Hollywood has always produced hundreds of movies while New York has produced thousands of books.

But not only are books more diverse in number; they are also more diverse in topic and character, and they are created for many different reasons. As a result of this defining feature of book publishing, book retailing is different from all other retailing.

But if the motivations behind the creation of those books are highly disparate, the motivations behind the purchase decisions are, if anything, even more so. Book retailing has to deal with an almost limitless selection of products. In fact, Amazon founder Jeff Bezos started with books because he saw that the vast selection that might appeal to any consumer constituted a severe challenge to stores with limited shelf and presentation space. He realized that putting search tools into the hands of the consumer would frequently present a shopping experience that was superior to in-store browsing.

# 2

# FROM IDEA TO BOOK

## What are agents and what do they do?

Agents, also sometimes called "literary agents," in the book business represent authors in their business interactions with publishers. The biggest publishers get nearly all their books through agents, so agents are effectively both scouts for new material and gatekeepers acting as editorial filters before publishers even see a work. They, not publishers, are the ones to whom fledgling authors go when they want to break into the industry. And it is extremely difficult to get the attention of major publishers without going through an agent. Compounding the challenge of breaking in for an aspiring author, it can be difficult to get the attention of a reputable agent. Some authors are lucky and get discovered by agents the same way that talent scouts might find models or actors, inspired by blogs, articles, or news coverage of authors-to-be. Others seek out agents to represent their work. Either way, they are connected, and the two parties have decided to work together (often meaning that they have signed a contract saying the agent will represent the author in question); their partnership begins with crafting what the agent will send the publisher.

Agents and authors work together on a book proposal or manuscript (usually a proposal) and then send it out to publishers. Publishers expect agents to give them professionally developed and vetted proposals and, ultimately, manuscripts. Active agents meet with publishers regularly—mostly with the acquisitions editors who actually spearhead the search for books for publishers but also, as appropriate, with marketing and sales staff as the agents' books move through the publishing process. They have extensive networks of editors and publishers and know just whom to contact when an exciting new project lands on their desk.

As authors' representatives, agents make the deals with publishers and negotiate the terms of the contracts. The biggest agents have negotiated their own unique "boilerplate" contracts with the biggest publishing houses, meaning they have made specific amendments to the publishers' contracts that can be called up any time the agency and publisher in question work together, without having to re-hash the terms. Book contracts cover a wide range of issues, and therefore, agents' changes to them do as well, from who gets to approve the cover design to who gets to sell the translation rights, and many questions in between. But the "deal" that is made comes down to royalties, advance, and rights, typically. The parties involved may go back and forth on these matters before they settle on what both can live with. And often there is competition involved; the agent will have shared the project with various publishers, and the publishers have to vie for projects with words, checks, attractive contract terms, and their prestige and brand. All of these facets of the publishing partnerships ahead can be explored as the agent works with the publisher or publishers to get the client (the author) the best possible deal and complete package.

What's in it for them? Agents make a percentage of what the publisher pays the author—typically 15 percent of the advance and subsequent royalties—but they get paid only if the book is sold to the publisher. They, like publishers and editors, also build up reputations and followings of their own, cultivating stables of authors that signal their strongest areas of publishing, their network of contacts, their eye for good projects, and their powers of persuasion.

With their commissions as incentives, agents are laser-focused on their mission to get authors the best deal they can for the books they represent and to ensure that they place projects with the publishers who will bring glory to their books. From the author's perspective, this work can be invaluable—it can be the difference between a book succeeding in finding a publisher and readers and not being read by anyone. But beyond these practicalities, the agent also can add a layer of value to the process of book publication. The best agents do not limit themselves to deals, for this reason.

Once the deal is done, agents also advise authors on all their interactions with the publisher throughout the development and publication of the book, and also later in the life of the book, if mediation between those parties is ever required. Additionally, agents review royalty statements for accuracy and process the payments from publishers, forwarding the author's share after deducting their agent commission.

As the publishing business has consolidated, particularly with big houses putting pressure on their editors to be expeditious, the time and bandwidth editors have for actually *editing* has diminished. That means that agents, who care deeply about the success their authors' books will achieve, are doing more editing to maintain quality. The agents' role in shaping the manuscripts has grown dramatically over the years. Agents work with authors on their proposals and their manuscripts. Agents' ability to add editorial value is part of why publishers are so much more comfortable acquiring from them than directly from authors who are not agented.

**What tactics can agents employ to make sure they get the most money for their clients when they sell rights to a publisher?**

Agents employ a variety of tactics when they sell manuscripts to publishers. Every agent uses most of these at one time or another, depending on what he or she thinks will work best for any particular book. An agent will start by identifying the editors most likely to be interested in the project being peddled. The next question is the submission strategy.

Sometimes an agent will rank the top editors most likely to pay the most for the book. Then the agent might go to the first two or three one by one, giving them an "exclusive" opportunity to read the proposal and consider it and take it off the market for a specific price the agent names. That approach leverages (and improves) the agent's relationship with those editors. It might also result in getting the editor to pay the price in order to avoid the possibility that multiple submissions might drive the price up.

Multiple submissions are also carefully controlled. When several editors get a proposal at the same time, they are usually made aware that the project is out to their competitors as well. This is meant to encourage a fast response. Once responses start, the dance begins. The interested editors want to take the project off the table. The agent wants to see if an "auction" can be created so that publishers will actually "bid" (usually in turn, sometimes just one "best bid") for the rights. And this whole game of three-dimensional tic-tac-toe is intricate when an author might have multiple book possibilities because it encourages complication: Will a publisher bid for two or three books at one time rather than one? The only limit to how complex this can all become is an agent's imagination (and, of course, a project that appeals to multiple potential buyers)!

### How does bidding work within publishing conglomerates?

Each of the big, multi-imprint houses has a protocol to deal with submissions that are made to more than one imprint, and what the bidding process is with in-house and with out-of-house competition.

Essentially the policies are designed to prevent two imprints from the same company being the only bidders in an auction or having more than one imprint from the same company in the final round. These situations would mean that instead of deciding inside the house on which imprint should publish the book, the total advance to the author would be determined using the conglomerate publisher's dollars bidding against itself.

Each big house has a different protocol for handling these situations, but common to all is preventing more than one imprint from the larger company being left in an auction in the last round of bidding. In many cases there is a competition of sorts in-house—how much each thinks they could spend if they were in an auction, the promotional plan they propose, sales strategies, and other considerations.

If the only imprints interested in the book when it comes to auction time are within the same house, the author and agent might have a say in which imprint wins, sometimes after a pitch by the remaining houses that outlines each contender's plans for the book.

### What does an acquiring editor do?

The acquiring editor in a publishing house finds the new projects for the house to publish. In general, acquiring editors "bring in" proposals for consideration by a larger group, or perhaps by one superior (an editor-in-chief or a publisher). Their decisions are not just based on what books seem interesting and likely to be popular but also on what they can afford given what they are permitted to spend on advances. Every house has different rules governing these things and frequently there are different rules for imprints within the same house.

Acquiring editors are usually responsible for projects from the moment they are signed up until they are published. The editor is the project's advocate within the house: first to get it signed and then to get it properly published. And, of course, the editor is the house's primary point of contact for the author and the author's agent.

It sometimes happens that acquiring editors have an idea for a book and then go out looking for a writer or writing team to execute it. But most books acquired by most publishers start from a proposal initiated by the author and submitted by an agent known to the acquiring editor.

### What does a publishing house need before offering a contract?

Most nonfiction books are acquired from a proposal describing the book and its audience, an outline or table of contents for the entire book, and a sample of the book's writing, which might be a couple of chapters.

For fiction from a debut author, more—perhaps the entire manuscript—would be required upfront for a house to make a purchase commitment so that they can see how strong the writing is throughout, how characters develop, and where the story goes.

In addition to the proposal describing clearly what the book will be, it will also describe the author's ability to help sell it. This will include a description of any "platform" the author has: ways he or she can communicate with potential readers (a blog, a newspaper column, or being in the public eye on any consistent basis). If the author has any friends or contacts in a position to promote the book who are willing to do so, that might also be mentioned in the proposal. Any other capabilities or plans the author has to get a book in front of its audience should also be featured in the proposal.

### How is a book's budget created and how is it used?

At the stage of assessing whether a publisher will pursue a given book project, various stakeholders at the publishing house have to assess the financial side of the book in question as well as its quality and suitability for them. Specifically, they have to come up with a budget for the book, known as a P&L, or profit and loss statement. To do this accurately, the editor or the editor's assistant gathers as much material on the book as possible. If it is a book by a house author (an author who has previously published with or currently has a contract with the publishing house), previous sales figures, reviews, and results from big accounts will all be taken into account; then ultimately a decision is made on whether to expect this book to do better or worse, in terms of sales, than other books by this author or other similar books that have been published.

If the author is new to the house but has published books with other publishers, the same happens, although the publisher will not have access to sales data as precise as if they had published the author's previous books themselves. In both cases the author's social media following and general level of popularity and fit with the topic of his or her proposed book are figured into the equation, although of course there are no algorithms for such calculations.

With a first book, or an author without a history at the house, there is more guessing involved than if there are plenty of hard data to draw from. On big books, or books that have likely retail outlets that are predictable in advance, a publisher will often solicit input on potential interest from its customer base before completing the P&L.

### How does the P&L factor into the publisher's decision to publish or not publish a book?

In the end, when the P&L is finished, the bottom line is compared to the house's norms and adjusted up or down as necessary to make it reasonable. Editors usually spearhead this process, but they must gather feedback from peers in other departments—crucially marketing, sales, and publicity departments—and gauge the level of enthusiasm about a project, as well as make sure that everyone is on board to support a certain advance and the sales expectations that underlie that advance figure. For example, if the publicity team expects it to be impossible to get media attention and review coverage of a book, it will be harder to justify projecting major sales, so the projections must be scaled down.

Editors also have to ask themselves, once the projected sales and revenue for a book have been sharpened with input from colleagues around the company, whether the expectations (a) meet those of the author and agent, or whether there is likely to be a disconnect there; and

(b) whether the scale of the book matches the amount of time and work the editor will need to put into it. Since (b) is a common, practical consideration for editors, agents who can deliver excellent, nearly ready-to-publish manuscripts are in a favored position versus other agents without that reputation. Let us look at some of the items that factor into the ever-important P&L.

### What is the publisher's retail price?

Although very few of a trade publisher's books are sold directly by the publisher to a final consumer, a price for that purpose always needs to be set. That is the publisher's retail price, or suggested retail price. It has long been established practice for trade publishers to print that price on the book's jacket or cover and, in general (even today), most stores usually sell most books at the prices marked by the publisher. And when the store is offering its customers a deal, selling the book at a price lower than the publisher's suggested retail, that "bargain" is clear to consumers because they can see the printed publisher's price.

The retail price is also the basis for the publisher's price to retailers or wholesalers, expressed as a "discount" off the retail price. For stores this is generally in the neighborhood of 45 percent off retail (so the store would "buy" a $20 book from a publisher for $11) and for wholesalers and very large retail accounts like Amazon or Barnes & Noble, the discount could be 50 percent off (or half the retail price) or even higher. In many author contracts, books sold at "excess discount," perhaps 60 percent off list or more, are treated differently when royalties are calculated.

In addition to the trade selling prices to retailer and wholesaler intermediaries being expressed as discounts "off list," the list price is the basis for royalty calculations in the big trade houses. Smaller publishers and hybrid publishers that publish non–trade books often base royalties on the "net amount received" rather than the retail price. Professional and academic publishers who often work this way frequently do not print their prices on the books. Because professional and academic houses can have a first printing that lasts for years, an unusual practice for a trade house, the ability to change price without being obvious about it (such as by stickering, which a trade house with a printed price would have to do) is an advantage. And with a far smaller percentage of the books sold in stores, the requirement for stores to "sticker" those books with a price for customers and cashiers is not as onerous.

### How do advances against royalties work?

To induce an author to sign a contract and to provide the author with an income that allows him or her time to write (because many, if not most, books are acquired on the basis of an outline and some sample writing, before they are completely written), publishers routinely give an author an "advance" payment. The amount of the advance is calculated based on how many copies the book is expected to sell. "Advances" are usually paid in stages against benchmarks of completion. So there might be a payment on signing, another when half the manuscript is turned in, another when the full manuscript is accepted, and even one sometimes "on publication." The advance constitutes a guaranteed minimum payment to an author as well, although on rare occasions, due to extenuating circumstances, an author must pay back his or her advance to the publisher. Advances paid for books for which an accepted manuscript follows are almost never subject to any clawback by the publisher.

Once a book is in the marketplace, publishers account— usually twice a year—to the author. Once the author's share of earnings from sales of books and rights exceeds what has been paid in the "advance against royalties," the publisher issues a check with the royalty statement for what the author is due.

### How do royalty rates vary by format and by publisher type?

Most publishers standardize their royalty rates by format. They pay different percentages for the hardcover, the trade paperback, the mass-market paperback, the e-book, and the audiobook. They also divide rights sales differently. Rights sales typically include sales to publishers in other countries and/or languages, or for "serial" publication (an excerpt in a magazine), or for a format (audio, perhaps, or something more unusual like a "promotional hardcover") that the originating publisher doesn't do.

Largely because they are working with hard-negotiating agents, big publishers' standard royalties are normally (and counterintuitively) higher than those paid by smaller houses. Large houses almost always base their volume royalty rates on the retail price; smaller houses frequently base it on the net money received by the publisher. This applies to royalty rates on export sales as well.

### How are the physical specifications for a new book determined?

In the industry, people refer to the dimensions of a book— its height and width across—as its "trim size." (This is not to be confused with "extent," which refers to the page count.) It used to be that for a trade hardcover title, or for a trade paperback, it seemed that an infinite number of trim sizes was available to the editor working with the book production or manufacturing department to devise a physical shell in which to house the new manuscript. Somehow, differences of half an inch, up or down, in a book's trim size were felt to give it an edge by making it somewhat unique in the sea of hardcovers it was to compete with on booksellers' shelves.

Trim size rationalization—in other words, reduction in the number of trim sizes available—was implemented industry-wide (over a *very* long period of time: decades beginning in the 1950s) as part of the trend toward reducing costs in manufacturing. Hardcover trim options came down from fifty or more variations, to about five key hardcover trim sizes, and at the same time brought significantly lower prices for the remaining trims. Estimating unit costs at specific volumes—2,500, 5,000, 10,000, and 25,000—became quicker and easier, and within a number of page ranges, these might be issued as precalculated schedules (volume price breaks usually appeared if these quantities were requested).

Author Mike Shatzkin's father, Leonard Shatzkin, introduced trim size rationalization at Doubleday in the 1950s. The company discovered that they were making books in a wide variety of trim sizes that were close to 5" x 8" and another wide variety that were close to 6" x 9", the two "standards" for trade books. Leonard Shatzkin mandated that the sizes would be uniform (probably 5 1/2" x 8 1/4" and 6 1/8" x 9 1/4", since those were the sizes that wasted the least amount of paper working from standard-sized "sheets"). At first this caused great internal distress, but ultimately people grew to understand that the difference of a quarter or eighth of an inch in any dimension was of importance or interest only to the book's designer. It was imperceptible to the reader, or even the editor!

As always, the first step is to have a cast-off done of the manuscript. This is a calculation of the anticipated page length at specific trim sizes and type fonts. This plus an estimate of how the book will bulk—how thick it will be—at different weights of paper give the editor a pretty good idea of what the book might look like and which price points will fit the package—particularly on very long or very short manuscripts.

The standard hardcover bestseller nowadays is 6" x 9" and an inch and a half in bulk, leading to that larger-than-life brick of a book sensation that writers of long works like Baldacci, DeMille, and others are given. Grisham runs even larger with a recent title at 6.4" x 9.3" x 1.6", a size that would qualify it as a possible murder weapon.

The literary hardcover used to telegraph its content to the reader by the use of a trim not so different from the big bestsellers, but enough to make a difference: 5¾" x 8¾" x 1, which was the trim on Nora Ephron's *Heartburn*, Patrick Suskind's *Perfume*, and *The Madonnas of Echo Park* by Brando Skyhorse.

Once the book's exterior trim is set, the editor has a variety of other variables to decide, and each adds to the overall unit cost. Some are visible to the consumer— printed end-papers, for example, are seen every time the book is opened. Others are less so, such as one-piece, three-piece, and full cloth cases.

The most visible and tactile choice, and often the one with the biggest impact on the unit cost, is the choice of the "sheet," or the type of paper, which is now almost always a free-sheet (acid free) of varying weight, opacity, color, texture, and bulking-thickness. It makes a difference to the consumer flipping through the book in the store, but the biggest impact is felt as the book is read. Whether it registers consciously, the heft of the paper can connote a book's gravitas.

### Do book jackets still impact sales?

Book covers still affect sales, though in a different way than they used to. Books by established fiction authors tend to have covers that are all about the type. Big block capitals, with the name of the author and the book's title so that you can read them from Mars. This helps in the retail selling environment but also online where most of them are sold. With probably 40 percent of the overwhelming Amazon sales being made on mobile devices, the clearer the jacket, the higher the sales are going to be. On books by new authors, we more often see evocative covers, some with strong type as well. In general, the effect is more artistic on these debut books, drawing in buyers visually, making them want to read about it online or pick it up at a bookstore. (In the heyday of book clubs when virtually all new-member advertising was full pages of postage stamp–sized book covers, hard-to-read covers were replaced with plain type that could be read easily.)

The use of fancy graphic enhancements on jackets—from UV coating that makes the cover shine, to simple embossing of the type to give a three-dimensional look and feel to the title or author's name, to embossing other graphic elements in the cover design—has always been expensive, and their impact on sales is unproven. If 60 percent of book sales are going to happen online, three-dimensional embellishments on a jacket will be replaced by animation that sells the book on Amazon, and jackets will get simpler.

### How is a book produced?

We will not go into detail on this process here, as the exact steps vary from house to house, but generally speaking, this much is true: the process begins with copyediting and then proceeds to the creation of page proofs, and authors and editors get the opportunity to check over both copy-edited pages and page proofs to make sure the book comes out as intended. A production editor oversees these processes and often both the production editor and copy editor are not in-house at the publishing house in question but rather work freelance (although to work for a publishing house they will have needed to prove their qualifications). Many publishers work with partner companies who provide production services for a wide range of companies. Others still have a more boutique-like approach. Among other things associated with managing the production process, production editors field questions and decide when they need to consult authors and editors, but there are standardized steps at which these parties are included in quality checks and other decisions.

The production of online products and e-books happens in parallel with that of print works so that the digital products reflect the same careful editing that is done on the print products, and coding for online publication can be integrated into the process early on.

### How do books get printed?

Book manufacturing expense remains the single biggest line item in the trade publisher's P&L, accounting for between 20 percent and 25 percent of costs when plant costs; paper, printing, and binding (PP&B); and inventory write-downs (the cost of books that are manufactured but not sold) are added up. When Penguin and Putnam merged in the mid-1990s they had several years of P&L gains from manufacturing savings that represented about 40 percent of the entire savings from the merger. In other words, the combined companies were able to print their books with a lower unit cost than the separate companies had before. This almost certainly had to do with better practices in one company being carried over to the output of the other.

Paper, of course, is a major component of the printing cost. Houses sometimes buy their own paper either to fit a consistent look and feel or to take advantage of purchasing economies of scale. But no publisher (since Doubleday sold its presses several decades ago) does its own printing, so the paper a publisher buys is "stored" with the company doing the actual printing.

Traditionally, printing companies have provided long offset print runs, with the publisher buying a first printing that minimizes unit cost and the demand it wants to be able to fill and then going back to press for reprints if the book is successful. But problems arise when the demand calculations are off. If you print 7,500 to get a significant break in the unit costs but end up selling only 1,000 copies, you've probably paid to warehouse half the units that never shipped, and then distributed the remaining copies and got the bulk back as very-expensive-to-process returns, which we discuss more in Chapter 3. And, in fact, sometimes overprinting results from yielding to the *temptation* of the lower unit cost or the requirement that a printing cost be at a certain level to enable a particular retail price. Those are cases where the rules publishers make to help them make money might actually cost money.

The temptation to overprint based on price breaks was recognized as a problem with a solution by an executive at Penguin in the early 1990s. Printing contracts were changed to charge a unit price based on the previous year's "average" print runs, so there was no evident price break for larger reprint quantities. This saved the production department from having to get multiple estimates for different reprint quantities and removed the temptation of overprinting because there was no price break for a larger quantity. As far as we know, that system remained in effect as long as Penguin was an independent company.

Recently, printers have started to offer digital printing options, churned out by fast ink-jet machines that can produce books with quality and appearance that match an offset copy. Here the unit costs do not go down with volume, but there are no minimum quantities; this means that publishers can print much closer to the demand. While unit costs might be higher, the effective unit costs when you figure in unused copies, cost of freight and warehousing, and other expenses often turn out to be lower.

### What is the average timeframe from a finished manuscript to a printed book?

For a variety of reasons, publication of a book usually still takes as much as a year—from creating galleys (which we discuss more in Chapter 3) early in production for publicity after publication, in order to allow plenty of time for popular revenue venues that are inundated with new books every day, to getting "preorders" from the public and "advance orders" from stores, and planning any publicity and marketing campaign that should occur when the book is published. Many of the marketing steps are expected to take place weeks or months in advance of the book's availability (such as presentation to major vendor accounts), so the timetable is as much mandated by marketing needs as by the time required to produce the book.

The publicity and marketing planning that is done most effectively when the manuscript is complete—both because then the house really knows what the book is and because at that point the publisher can plan the publication schedule without the variable of how long it will take the author to finish writing—means there is little incentive in most houses to speed up production. Ordinarily, a book has to be copy-edited, which changes it in ways the author must see and approve. Then it is "set" in type—which today means "made to look as it will when it is a book," and the author generally reviews it again.

Although publishers discourage changes made after the approved manuscript is in production, authors still make them. So there may be more than one "pass" between the house and the author between completed copyediting and a designed book ready for a printer. If the book is "complex"—illustrated or with art, which could be charts or graphs, integrated in any way—it will take longer.

And if a book is indexed, that step has to be done last, when the page numbers of all the content are settled.

### What are subsidiary rights?

Publishers are responsible for squeezing all the revenue they can out of an author's book. All publishers are expected to be set up to handle the principal publication of the book as a whole, often called "volume rights," and for that the royalties are paid on sales according to the contract. But there are other ways to get revenue that depend on apparatus outside most publishers' expertise and organizational capability. These rights are "licensed" by the publisher as "subsidiary rights" and the revenue received for those rights is divided with the author by percentages spelled out in the author's contract.

Most rights revenue for books falls into standard buckets: book clubs, other print editions (paperback), and foreign (English in another country or another language). Publishers have staff who sell those rights and maintain regular contact with the most established entities that buy them.

Agents, of course, start out controlling the entire package of "rights" for any project and the publisher gets to exploit only those rights that the agent has granted in the book contract. Some rights, like the right to be sold by major book clubs, are almost never split out. Book clubs dodged pricing laws when they were created because they licensed rights, rather than buying books, and printed their own editions. Over time, this distinction was elided, but when clubs don't print their own and buy from the publisher's run, they still often buy the books at a "manufacturing cost" and then add a "royalty" for the full price. And they often don't pay the royalty price if they don't sell the inventory to an end user. So the distinction between how book clubs buy and how other retailers buy remains.

Other rights, like most foreign rights in countries other than Canada, are often held by the agent or, in some cases, sold before an English-language publisher gets at the project. (Not everything originates in English.) Rights might also be sold to use part of the book in some way, in a magazine or a collection of material including some from other books; these are called "first serial rights" if the portion in question is published first in such a venue, as a way of drumming up interest for the book that is appearing soon. And rights can be sold for uses as unusual as toilet paper.

The various book fairs held around the world—the biggest and most prominent being the Frankfurt International Book Fair held each year, usually in October—represent concentrated opportunities for trading rights across languages and countries. Publishers either go to Frankfurt or get their rights represented by somebody else who goes, either an agent or one of a number of services that will take books to book fairs.

Now that we've laid out some of the basics of the early life of a book—the agent's role, the editor's work in acquiring the book, the publishing houses' calculations of profits and losses, and other key concepts you need to understand—let's look at what happens to books when they go out into the world, on the journey from publishers to readers.

# 3

# BOOKSELLING, MARKETING, AND SALES

## GETTING THE BOOK TO THE READER

*How does a book go from a publisher to a reader?*

Trade publishers, who are the biggest, the best known, and the focus of this book, are called that because they sell primarily through the book "trade," which is bookstores, libraries, and the wholesalers—intermediaries that stock books from many publishers—that serve them. Things have changed in the past twenty years because of the internet and the ability of publishers to address consumers individually in ways they never could in the past, but trade publishers still primarily reach consumers through "intermediaries"—the bookstores and the libraries.

*How do publishers view "the trade"?*

Publishers are primarily interested in bookstores. Today that also means online retailers, mainly Amazon.com, but also BN.com, the online sales arm of the bookstore chain Barnes & Noble. B&N is the biggest brick-and-mortar account, and they compete with the book departments of mass merchants like Costco and Walmart as well as with hundreds, or perhaps over a thousand, viable "independent" bookstores.

All of these stores need to be "covered" by sales representatives who pitch each individual book title to a buyer for each store (chain buyers buy for many stores, of course) in advance of its appearance, using a catalog and a book jacket to "present" the title. Stores routinely order books before they're printed to arrive as soon as they are printed. These are the "advance orders": the books in place for purchase on the official publication date (about a month after books ship). That's when reviews are to run and books are in place for consumers to buy.

### How do publishers typically see and then serve their customer base?

Publishers sell to a variety of accounts and organize their sales departments to maximize their effectiveness and manage their costs of coverage.

Dedicated book retailers include chains, the biggest of which are Barnes & Noble and Books-a-Million, and independent stores. Publishers tell us there are from 500 to 800 of them in the country that really count. National account teams based at headquarters cover the chains, and a field sales force—often augmented these days by telemarketers—covers the independents. Field representatives, or reps, can be dedicated and employed by the house or they can be "commission" reps who sell for a number of publishers. Many smaller publishers work through larger entities for distribution. Ingram Publisher Services, owned and operated by the industry's biggest wholesaler, is the largest of those. All of the major houses offer distribution services to selected publishers and there are a few competitors to Ingram; Independent Publishers Group is probably the largest, but there is also National Book Network. The distribution services include not just sales but also warehousing, fulfillment, and collection of receivables. Some publishers buy physical distribution services from a larger player and then do their own sales effort. Accounts don't want to maintain relationships with too many different warehouses because it adds an administrative burden to an already complex logistical business.

Ingram and Baker & Taylor (B&T) are the two national wholesalers with multiple warehouses. They serve libraries and institutions and they also provide stores with a way to order the books of several or many publishers at one time for consolidated delivery. Therefore, they are often used for reorders of books that were initially ordered directly from a publisher. There are also local wholesalers, although they have diminished in number and importance. Publishers generally handle the national wholesalers with their national sales staff, but it is not unheard of for the reps who are local to the wholesalers' home offices to be the publisher's main point of contact with them.

Mass merchants who sell books, including Costco, Walmart, Target, and others, are often reached through specialty wholesalers and are usually handled by publishers' national account teams. These accounts generally move big quantities of a smaller number of titles with a higher percentage of returns than publishers see from independent stores or even from bookstore chains.

Libraries tend to buy from wholesalers. Whereas many publishers offer no discount incentive for libraries to buy directly from them, the wholesalers offer a range of other services libraries want around making books shelf-ready. Publishers do promote directly to the libraries and are comfortable selling to them through the wholesale channels.

Retailers and other sellers, like mail order or web catalogs, who sell books as a sideline to other merchandise that is more central to them, are increasingly important accounts, particularly to nonfiction publishers. These nonbook retailers are considered "special sales" accounts. They often buy without the right of return, but in those cases usually at discounts higher than those the book trade gets. Generally, publishers succeed with special sales accounts because they have a body of content that complements the accounts' main line of merchandise. Gardening books, home repair books, and knitting books, as examples, have natural homes in specialty stores. Sometimes consolidators or specific wholesalers specialize in those books for those accounts. The "special sales department" generally works from a publisher's home office.

### What is the history of allowing booksellers to return unsold inventory?

"Returns" are the convention by which a publisher's bookstore and wholesaler customers may send back unsold copies of a book and have most or all of the purchase price credited to their account. (It is generally accepted that the practice spread during the Depression, when it became increasingly difficult to get bookstores to take risks on new books.)

In most cases, the store or wholesaler will have paid the shipping cost to bring the books in and, in nearly all cases, will pay the shipping cost for sending them back. In addition, the account will have paid the publisher for those unsold books, so it will have had its cash tied up in that inventory. And there is labor involved both in receiving and shelving and then pulling and packing books for return. So stores have plenty of incentive to minimize returns. Nonetheless, trade book returns generally are 20 to 30 percent of a publisher's shipments. That's an average. When it happens that very high sales expectations are met with a lack of audience interest, an individual title's returns can be much higher than that. Titles with 50 percent returns are not uncommon, and titles for which everything goes wrong could result in returns of 80 percent or more.

Overall, returns are highest on heavily advanced new titles and they are lowest on backlist. Backlist returns of 20 percent to 30 percent would be excessive. Part of the reason that backlist is seen as "more profitable" is because the sales are made with far fewer returns.

Overall, returns have gone down as sales have shifted from retail stores to Amazon. Amazon's returns are lower, probably without exception, than other retail accounts. Generally, the accounts that sell bigger numbers of fewer titles (like mass merchants) have higher returns and those that stock a broader array of titles, including a lot of backlist (like independent stores), have lower returns.

During the Depression, the returns option became practically universal among trade houses. Although publishers perennially complain about returns, they are actually indispensable. Returns enable bookstores to take risks stocking titles on which they have no sales history and for which they have only the publisher's conviction as an indicator that the book will sell. And they enable stores to get inventory dollars back to reinvest in different books when something they've ordered doesn't sell. And returns also prevent markdowns from a store that over-ordered a title that can hurt the sales or reputation of a store that didn't and is selling the book at the normal price. Allowing returns is also an acknowledgment that bookselling is not an exact science, with every new title a new "product" to sell.

### Has any publisher tried to eliminate returns?

The only attempt we can recall by a general trade publisher to eliminate returns was by Harcourt Brace Jovanovich in the early 1980s. They introduced a new discount schedule that gave booksellers *much* higher discounts than were normal in the trade but without the right of return. The reception by booksellers to the attempt was so chilly that it was withdrawn very quickly; it didn't last one full season.

One way of "mitigating" returns that has stuck was invented by New American Library, a paperback house with a hardcover list in the late 1970s. They introduced 46/53, by which they gave stores a 46 percent discount for purchases (substantially higher than the 40–42 percent prevailing at that time) but credited returns at only a 53 percent discount. The calculation was that stores would get pretty much normal discounts if their returns were 20 percent and be gaining margin over the normal terms if their returns were lower than that. Variations of this strategy, essentially offering something less than a full credit for the purchase upon return, have stuck and are part of many publishers' terms today.

### How do publishers know what books will be popular and which will not?

For years, people from outside the book business would look at what we did and wonder, "Don't you do any market research on what you publish?" There were a lot of explanations for why we didn't, but they often boiled down to one cold hard fact: "The first printing is the market research." Until a book is out and available for sale, and people either seize the opportunity to make the book their own or completely ignore it—as there is no in between—you really can't know how a certain book will fare.

Of course, in the internet era it is now *possible* to do market research, or, more precisely, audience research, very economically, and it can better inform publishers' guesses. For a couple hundred dollars in effort, publishers can get very useful data on audience sizing and segmentation, how accessible these potential buyers are online, and what search terms and hash tags you'd have to optimize to reach the audience. If you have a sense of who your target readers are and what they're interested in, modern digital marketing research can tell you where to find them and what they search for. This is a sea change. We have gone from a world where market research costs just didn't fit the problem to one where it is foolish to skip the market research step.

Despite that, as this is being written, audience research is not yet a standard practice across publishing, even across the big houses.

### What do the sales, publicity, and marketing departments of publishing houses do?

The "sales department" primarily interacts with the intermediaries that put the publishers' books into actual readers' hands. They promote books directly to those accounts and manage the various sales programs a publisher uses to encourage the stocking of the books.

The "publicity department" of a publisher—often a small unit housed within an imprint—works with media to push awareness of the publisher's books. This function includes getting the books reviewed through all media, some of which (like *Publishers Weekly*) review books before publication and most (like newspapers) when the book is available. It also includes pushing author appearances through radio and TV and press interviews.

The "marketing department" really supports sales and coordinates other efforts with publicity. The marketing department is responsible for advertising and making the overall decisions about the spending on marketing and its coordination with sales efforts.

Because of the internet and the ability to reach consumers directly, the marketing function has grown over the past couple of decades. In many houses, we see sales departments cut (because there are fewer accounts) and marketing departments growing. Marketing is also increasingly involved in direct contact with accounts. Online sales is arguably more a marketing function than a sales function, considering the historical skill sets for those departments.

There is also a lot of variation in how publishers' sales teams treat different books. Each book is weighted according to target audience, price, potential for publicity, and other factors to determine which of the sales channels it fits best: traditional book accounts on-land, traditional book accounts online, libraries, schools, Big Box and specialty retail stores, the price and warehouse clubs, other channels.

### When does book marketing begin?

The marketing of a book can begin the moment the book is signed by a house, and at times it does. Other times, the publisher might delay marketing efforts to enable more development of the book and a clearer understanding of the potential audience. But in almost all cases, individual title marketing begins many months and perhaps a year before the book is published. Sometimes this work is merely "audience identification" to enable better targeting. But sometimes, in the internet age, publishers will start "teasing" a book's forthcoming appearance to online audiences long before publication. This is increasingly the case because preorders—orders from actual end-user consumers placed before the book comes out—are a relatively new feature of the internet age and a very important one. A book's initial sale influences its chances of becoming a bestseller, and preorders boost the initial sale.

## Has the internet had a noticeable impact on publishers' marketing practices?

From our vantage point, a bit over two decades after Amazon.com opened for business a couple of years before Google was born, *everything* in publishing has changed since the advent of the internet.

By the year 2000, even before there were measurable e-book sales, the share of print sales taking place online began to change publishers' marketing focus. There was now not only a point to marketing books directly to consumers regardless of what the inventory position was with the retailers, but there were tools for marketing that had never existed before. Publishers could address consumers directly through Amazon. But the awareness of how cheap and effective email could be had also begun to grow. And then online searching (referred to colloquially as "search") also started to grow in obvious importance. So it became possible to do a lot of effective and inexpensive marketing that resulted in actual sales, without regard to what the sales department was doing. And without regard to what the inventory on store shelves was.

Publishers are becoming increasingly sophisticated about doing audience research and understanding who the likely buyers of a book are and how to reach them with the right message at the right time. Social media and targeted advertising based on browsing and shopping habits take the middlemen—sales departments and brick-and-mortar stores—out of the equation, help publishers cultivate more curated and intimate relationships with their customers, and also constantly feed data back to their marketing departments so they can continue to fine-tune their ways of getting people to buy books and, in general, help promote their brands. But what is most critical about the internet is that it has organized the world into microgroups of interest. For the first time, publishers are looking at market divisions that are more granular than the books they publish. If you have a book for left-handed third-grade teachers who once taught in a suburb and now teach in a city, to make up an example, you can find them and target them with messages. That was never possible before. Since books are often aimed at very specific audiences, this ability to target so precisely is of more use to book publishers than it is to media that require bigger audiences per product for commercial viability.

Publishers have for years distributed printed copies of the books that were from type that was set but not a final version. These were called "bound galleys," a term that is a relic of the long-ago days of hot-metal typesetting when the type was delivered in trays called "galleys" before it was "made up" into "pages," the typographic presentation of the book itself.

Of course, galleys today might not be printed; they might be electronic or "e-galleys" instead. There has been a service for more than a decade called NetGalley, which makes it easy and much cheaper than it would otherwise be to distribute physical proofs to get the book in front of potential reviewers. But there are still plenty of printed galleys, or advance copies, distributed to reviewers and store buyers. Publication dates still are set, although more modern distribution techniques make it much easier to achieve a "simultaneous national laydown," where books arrive in most stores at about the same time.

Now, "discovery," raising consumer awareness of books, has moved from happening primarily in bookstores to happening primarily on the web. That has shifted this critical function from a subsection of the sales department—because this department puts the books in the stores—to a digital marketing challenge that may have little or nothing to do with account relationships.

On the other hand, discovery also occurs because of the actions of the retailers—whether they put a book in a window or a featured spot on a front table, or even whether they put it into the right store section—and those relationships are still owned by the sales department. So in the modern era, we have marketers concentrating heavily on direct-to-consumer messages and sales departments managing marketing activities through accounts like Amazon's and Barnes & Noble's online efforts.

As a result, the roles and functions of marketing and sales are undergoing change, a process that is playing out right now. This is an extremely complicated dance, made more so by the fact that sales in big houses is almost always a centrally managed function and most marketing activity takes place "in the imprints," so marketing "leadership" is scattered around the house. Different houses come up with different responses to this change in circumstances, and we already see differences both within and among houses in how marketing is handled.

### What is the role of the sales representative?

Sales representatives, known as sales reps, originally had a simple, clear, and defined function. They "presented" new titles to bookstore buyers, who would then determine whether to carry a book and, if they did want to carry it, how many copies to order for their stores. Reps also encouraged the stocking of backlist titles in stores and, of course, served as the frontline customer service representative of the house with the accounts.

As the number of bookstore accounts to call on has diminished, the rep role has been somewhat redefined. Almost all publishers have added telemarketing sales forces to complement the role of the field reps so that accounts can get more frequent attention with fewer traveling reps in the field. Penguin Random House a few years ago created a program called Rep 2.0, which gave reps responsibility for such things as presentations at schools and businesses. This was intended to use their title knowledge to the house's marketing advantage and enable the house to maintain a larger force while competitors were cutting back. That approach appears not to have been copied by other houses.

### Why do some houses outsource sales and others do not?

Two short answers: cost and management. You have to be of a certain minimum size to afford your own sales force. Few houses are large enough. And running a sales force requires a lot of management attention and bandwidth.

Because just about every sales force owner (publishers and a few distributors) wants more volume to support the sales force cost, any publisher can access a complete sales team without owning it. The advantage is that the publisher or distributor avoids the cost commitment and the management responsibility. You swap fixed costs for variable costs. The disadvantage is that each one has to compete for the sales force's attention; no individual user owns it.

### What are preorders and why do they matter?

Encouraging preorders by consumers—orders for the book that ship the moment the book is available—has become a standard practice. This encourages behavior that is almost precisely the opposite of what was the conventional wisdom about book marketing for decades until very recently. Earlier, publishers assiduously avoided targeted consumer efforts on a book before publication date. Just as it was considered pointless to expend effort or money pushing a book that was not currently in full bookstore distribution, it made no sense to anybody to push a book before it was out and available for a consumer to buy. In fact, the concept of a "publication date" originally was to guide media outlets about when was the right time to publish a review. In days past when many stores got their books from publishers via slow mail, books would ship to stores over the weeks before the publication date so all the stores had the books on that date. It was a mutual interest of publishers and review media to hold the review for the publication date. The publishers got the most efficient sales assistance if the review ran only when books were widely available. And the media also served its readers best by reviewing books only when those who read the review could readily get the book. But this has completely changed with online shopping and the move toward pre-orders. In part, this is consumer-driven, but it also serves the publishers' interest.

It has long been important to publishers to get a big "first week" sale for each new book because that gives the book the best odds of making a bestseller list. Publishers didn't want that first week sale spread out over a longer time period, and that was another reason they tried to aim publicity and full distribution at a particular publication date. As online sales have grown as a percentage of the total sale, it now makes sense to build that number by giving consumers more time, which now sometimes could be months, to place orders that would all ship in that first week. So months and months of preordering can accumulate to deliver the illusion of banner sales made in the first week, helping the book make a bigger splash when it finally comes out. For this reason, publishers now make books available to preorder online far in advance of their publication date. This gets readers excited about highly anticipated releases and gives the publisher real consumer feedback from an early stage, providing a barometer of how successful a book is going to be and at the same time increasing a book's chances of making the bestseller lists. And hitting the bestseller lists is something authors and publishers will trumpet for years, even if a book is on the list only briefly before being overtaken by the next big thing.

### How do books get to bookstores and the supply chain?

Bookstores receive books either directly from publishers or from a trade wholesaler. Most stores will still order the first copies of most books directly from publishers as an "advance order" placed with a sales rep before the books are ready. The books are usually published in seasonal "lists," or groupings, two or three per year. The sales reps theoretically get to all their accounts before the first titles on any list ship, so stores have a chance to order upcoming titles for delivery when they're published. In this way, new titles are "pushed" out to the stores.

Backlist, on the other hand, is more often a result of stores "pulling." After the reps take orders for the initial shipments, the impetus for reordering those books and older ones generally under current practices must come from the stores, almost all of them assisted by computerized inventory-tracking systems. Publishers do occasionally try to inspire backlist orders by offering special deals for backlist ("dated billing," where you get books today but don't get billed for them for a few months, is one such technique), but for the most part stores order what books they want and when they think they need them.

We would interject here that we are reporting pretty much universal practice, but not what we would necessarily consider "best" practice. Mike's father, Leonard Shatzkin, introduced a different way to sell backlist in 1955, by which Doubleday automated backlist replenishment for the stores in response to inventory counts the reps reported after their visits. This technique propelled Doubleday from one of many publishers to an industry leader, particularly for backlist. Over time, different management allowed the system to atrophy and computerization led stores to be more confident that their own ordering was efficient.

But the fact is that the titles that sell only one copy in any month in a store will be the vast majority of titles that sell any copies at all. Only chains have a broader view across multiple stores that would enable them to distinguish which among those titles should be replenished based on current sales trends and which not. Independent stores would benefit from publishers automating these decisions with their much bigger base of knowledge. But this has not happened. Instead, stores rely heavily on aggregate sales from Ingram reporting what they are shipping. (The logic is that current shipments by the biggest wholesaler are a good proxy for measuring current movement of a book out of stores.) Recently a systems vendor called Above the Treeline has allowed its participating stores to get a cumulative view of title sales across the user base. These are very useful pieces of data for an isolated independent trying to figure out what to reorder from its own sales data. Publishers also solicit orders in advance from wholesalers as they do with stores. And they are also generally content to have the reorders go through the wholesalers, even though it reduces the publishers' margin.

Trade publishers also sell books through retailers that aren't bookstores and through any other channel, like direct mail catalogs, they can find. Those sales outside the book trade are usually called "special sales." Special sales have become increasingly important to trade publishers as bookstore shelf space has shrunk.

### How do publishers pay to buy prominence in online retailers, and brick-and-mortar stores?

Retailers of all kinds, not just in books, recognize that they can "sell" premium placement of a suppliers' goods within their ecosystem. These transactions often take place within the context of a "co-op advertising allowance." When this started in the book business decades ago, it was the way publishers helped stores subsidize local print advertising. The convention was that publishers would allocate a co-op budget based on purchases, sometimes a cumulative number of dollars transferred between the publisher and the store and sometimes based on the order for a particular title. Then the publisher would pay for a percentage of advertising costs for "approved" titles against that budget.

Part of what drove that historical use of co-op was that most newspapers had "local rates." So the bookstore in a town could get a better price on the space ad from the local daily than a publisher could coming in from the outside. Co-op advertising, subsidized by the publisher but actually bought locally by the store, gave the publisher the benefit of the local pricing.

Over the years, store placement has evolved as the most effective marketing tool, with far more impact than any local print advertising. (Indeed, even in the days when print advertising was important, the placement in store a publisher knew it would get because it was supporting the ad was part of the expectation.) Brick-and-mortar stores put a price on prime display space like front tables or end caps—for example, the octagon table at the front of any Barnes & Noble store. And online stores put a price on featured placement of a title in response to searches or in association with other titles. Normally, the amount the publisher is on the hook for is some percentage of what the store buys from them, cumulatively.

### What are a publisher's terms of sale?

Every publisher has standard "terms of sale" that are published and spell out the basis on which it will sell books to its most standard intermediaries: bookstores, libraries, wholesalers, and special sales accounts. The stated terms include the *discount off the retail price* that will be allowed (often based on the size of the order: the number of books being ordered), whether or not returns of unsold inventory are allowed, whether the publisher or the customer will pay the freight to transport the books to the account, and how much time from invoicing will be allowed before payment is expected. Although each publisher's terms are "unique," they tend to be fairly similar, all the more so because they are published and everybody can see everybody else's.

It is permissible for publishers to have contractual private terms with any account, and that is the basis of most transactions between the largest publishers and their largest accounts. But the published terms of sale are prevalent for most publishers with most accounts.

### What mainstream digital marketing techniques have been adopted by publishing?

Remarketing is a ubiquitous internet marketing technique by which any online retailer places a digital "cookie" to identify any visitor to its site; it can work with a Google advertising program that follows the visitor to other sites that have carved out space for Google advertising, so that space is then used to re-promote a product from the initial site. In the case of books—as with other products—it can be disconcerting to be browsing the Web, only to find two or three sites after you've been on Amazon or BN.com showing an ad for the book or books you'd just spent time browsing or searching for. Over time, however, consumers have grown more and more accustomed to this phenomenon for all sorts of products they shop for online.

The programs can run for some time depending on what other ads are bidding to appear in the space where the book remarketing will show up. In the end, it comes down to the principle of not giving up, of repeat exposure to something you've already expressed interest in. If you click the item to reconsider, you are back on the online retailer's page and can buy the specific remarketed book or something else on the site.

The same is true of "cart" marketing, where the online retailer will remind you by email one or more times about the items you've left in your shopping cart—known as cart abandonments—and perhaps even offer you a small 10 percent or 15 percent discount to complete the checkout process.

The shift over the past twenty years to an online world where book customers learn about their books and often transact for them virtually has spawned the innovative—almost certainly transitional—world we live in today. But the business is still largely shaped by its history, which we now give a closer examination.

# 4

# SOME PUBLISHING HISTORY

*When were today's major publishing houses founded?*
Although it was evolving, the trade book publishing business had remained largely the same for the first hundred years or so of the republic, until about a fifty-year period starting with the last quarter of the nineteenth century. During that time, many of the companies were founded that still—under the names of (all) the men who created them—make up big pieces of the book publishing industry today (although some of the enduring imprint names, as you will see, go back to the early part of the nineteenth century).

Harper & Row was founded in New York in 1817, while William Collins was launched in London in 1819. These venerable houses (or rather their direct descendants) were combined in 1990, to beget today's mega-publisher HarperCollins.

Similarly, the Hachette Book Group is the sum of Little Brown & Company, begun in Boston in 1837, and Warner Books, which began its life in publishing in 1970 when it acquired the Paperback Library (founded in 1961).

The nineteenth century ended with Frank Nelson Doubleday Sr. founding Doubleday & McClure with Samuel McClure in 1897 (Theodore Roosevelt Jr. is said to have been a vice president of the company briefly). This venture morphed into Doubleday, Doran with the addition of George H. Doran to the team in 1927.

With the end of World War I came the influx of an energetic cadre of publishing talent whose names still dominate book spines to this day: Blanche and Alfred Knopf founded Alfred A. Knopf Inc. in 1915; Richard L. Simon and M. Lincoln Schuster graduated from Columbia and founded Simon & Schuster in 1924; and Bennett Cerf and Donald Klopfer began Random House in 1927 after first acquiring the Modern Library. Four other reading powerhouses that dominated the twentieth century were founded in the 1920s: Henry Luce brought *Time* magazine to life in 1923, the Wallaces started *Reader's Digest* in 1922, Harry Sherman founded Book-of-the-Month in 1926, and Nelson Doubleday's company began the Literary Guild in 1927. The book clubs offered the increasingly busy consumer a pre-selected sampling of the best new books available. Their books represented self-betterment or continuing education delivered to your door, enabling the busy workingman or woman to keep up with the culture of the day as chosen by these companies. The publishers served as curators, as they do today. Their stamp of approval on written works was required for book clubs to consider them.

### How did the modern "book trade" evolve?

When the twentieth century began, there were very few bookstores and libraries. Many books were sold by "subscription." Publishers' representatives literally went door to door soliciting orders. General Grant's memoirs were a big success in the 1880s because there were so many veteran Union soldiers available for publisher Mark Twain to recruit to go out and do the solicitations!

In the early part of the twentieth century, bookstores willing to invest in inventory and libraries, most funded by Andrew Carnegie, began to form a "book trade." And publishers began to hire sales reps to visit the libraries and other book outlets. After World War I, publishers began to "cover" bookstores in the way that we think about it now, with traveling representatives making a serious effort to visit all significant bookstore accounts every publishing "season" so that new books were "fully distributed" when they were published.

Richard L. (Dick) Simon was the co-founder of Simon & Schuster (S&S) with his Columbia University classmate, Max Schuster, who made a habit of hanging out with booksellers. It was Schuster who first suggested they might discount S&S's books, and also, in 1925, he offered the booksellers the privilege of returning unsold copies for credit as a way to entice orders from their company which was only one year old at the time.

### What led to the rise of paperbacks and what were its effects?

On the eve of World War II, the first rumblings were felt of the seismic shift that would impact virtually all areas of the publishing business and radically change the consumer book-reading behavior that drives it. While Germany had experimented with efficient trim sizes on their paperbacks, it was Allen Lane in the United Kingdom who launched the Penguin books imprint in 1935. To get the books for Penguin, he bought paperback reprint rights. Sales, sluggish at first, were saved by a large order from Woolworths. In 1939, S&S partnered in another paperback experiment called Pocket Books, which was very successful, giving S&S its powerful paperback arm and giving readers the generic name for all mass-market paperbacks, which are also known just as "mass-markets."

It is in the postwar history of the paperback that we see the publishing industry, and its readership, behave very much as they would fifty-plus years later when faced with the advent of the digital book.

The paperback revolution was enabled by using an entirely new (to books) distribution channel: the mass-market IDs (independent distributors) who placed reading material with newsstands and other accounts that would not make title-by-title decisions about what to stock. This ability to "force distribution" was coupled with returns of "covers only," which were picked up by the ID's detail reps and had no real "cost" to the retail outlet.

But this kind of distribution also favored "categories": mysteries, romances, westerns, and science-fiction as well as already branded "bestsellers" that were licensed for the purpose from their original hardcover publishers. The ubiquitous presence of these books very much broadened the market; the new readers were "category" readers, quite different from the title-by-title shoppers who bought books previously only in bookstores and department store book departments.

### How did the paperback industry evolve after World War II?

After the war, a number of exclusively paperback publishing houses were founded to exploit the new ID-driven distribution channel with the more genre-related titles that were selling like crazy in the format. These paperback readers showed a taste for category publishing—romance, westerns, mystery, science fiction—and so an entirely new subset of publishing was born. Aside from a completely different distribution method and the genre specialization it required, there were differences in the publishing economics from trade practices: the royalties paid were different (sometimes the mass-market authors were work-for-hire with no royalties), manufacturing costs and minimum print quantities were different, and the mass-market industry in the first ten or fifteen years after World War II had very little focus on "backlist," which didn't lend itself to the big number laydown distribution method that made mass-market publishing work. The new rack-sized mass-markets had a lasting home in train stations, but they also started to appear displayed in other nontraditional book venues like drugstores. Soon bookstores also had mass-markets in racks.

Mike Shatzkin worked in the brand-new paperback department of New York's biggest bookstore, Brentano's on 5th Avenue, in 1962. At that time, the trade paperbacks were bought like hardcovers by the store's buying staff. But the mass-markets were still controlled by the sales reps from the mass-market houses, increasingly cutting the IDs out of the most lucrative and lowest-returns accounts. This ultimately left the IDs with the highest-return, least-profitable accounts, through which the growing number of mass-market publishers tried to move more and more titles and higher and higher quantities. Ultimately, by the 1980s, this led to the ID channel becoming progressively less efficient. Today it hardly exists.

### How did the bookstore network evolve over the years since World War II?

There have been five distinct periods of growth for bookstores. In the first, from the end of World War II until the early 1960s, independent bookstores and department store book sections benefited from the increases in literacy and affluence that drove growth in publishers and publishing. So even while mass-market paperbacks were introducing what might be seen as competition for stores and trade books, trade book sales grew and so did the outlets carrying them.

Then in the 1950s and 1960s, the second stage, shopping malls were developed. Mall developers wanted chains to occupy their store slots because they were more bankable. That led to the growth of the mall bookstore chains, B. Dalton and Waldenbooks, which built relatively small, ten-thousand- to fifteen-thousand-title stores for those venues. By the early 1970s, each of them had hundreds of outlets.

Part of the reason that department stores were the most important component of the retail network until the 1960s was because they had systems to deal with many SKUs (the acronym meaning "stock keeping units," which in this case means the discrete book titles the store has to keep track of) and to buy from many vendors, a requirement for stocking books effectively. Then when the big shopping mall build-out gathered steam in the 1950s and 1960s, the development of malls spawned the retail chains Walden and Dalton. Mall developers just wanted "bankable" tenants, but that requirement created specialty chains.

The B. Dalton chain was the first big operation to start capturing point-of-sale data. This was done before each book reliably carried an identifying number on it; the ISBN (International Standard Book Number) was invented in the 1960s and it took some time before its display on books became universal. So Dalton created their own SKU numbers and affixed them to each book with a sticker. This extra processing step was expensive, but it enabled real inventory control across the chain.

The inventory control stickers allowed Dalton to create the concept of "model stock," books that would automatically be reordered when they sold. This happened about 1970; it enabled the first massive leap forward in bookselling efficiency and was of particular value in keeping a backlist of enduring interest in stores.

This move gave Dalton a big competitive advantage. Other stores might not have been able to keep up, except for another tech breakthrough that occurred in the early 1970s.

Stage three occurred because in the early 1970s, Ingram, which had been a relatively unimportant local wholesaler in Tennessee, put their inventory onto a microfiche so that stores could see before they ordered what books they'd get. This revolutionized the ability of independent stores to compete with chains and sparked a new period of independent store growth, with a concomitant increase in publishers' ability to sell backlist titles.

Next came stage four, discounting, sparked by the Crown Bookstore chain in the 1980s. Crown's formula was to stock only a handful of really current trade books and to sell them at a discount off the publishers' suggested (and printed on the book) price. The bestsellers were sold at loss-leader, almost-no-margin prices, and the other trade titles stocked went for lesser discounts. The store's inventory consisted mostly of remainders and "bargain books," either previously published or not-really-trade books that were always sold at lower prices.

Stage five appeared shortly thereafter, when the big chains (Walden and Dalton) and Wall Street both discovered that massive 100,000-plus title stores were magnets for book readers that didn't require a mall for placement. They were inspired by a Texas outlet called BookStop that used a version of the Crown discounting strategy along with a massive selection as a winning formula. Soon that became the strategy as well for Barnes & Noble (which bought B. Dalton) and Borders (which bought Walden). By the mid-1990s, these stores were ubiquitous and, with indies (independents) and mall store networks also still largely intact, they marked the high-water mark of shelf space for book publishers to fill in retail outlets.

Then came Amazon . . .

We are now about ten years into the time of the digital book. And while the changes playing out are a mix of the obvious and the surprising, the initial impact on the consumer publishing business bears most resemblance to the paperback revolution and its impact on mainstream editions, on pricing, royalties, expanded markets, and the ability to increasingly source and deliver books to specific audience niches.

The other transforming change for the business is how each publisher deals with the avalanche of new consumer sales and other related behavioral data. For many in our industry this new information will represent their first contact with objective data about their books and the masses.

# 5

# E-BOOKS

Although much of the e-book market and world is in flux, one thing is safe to say: the success of e-books is difficult for publishers and resellers to predict, and it has been from the beginning. If there is one thing the publishing establishment has failed to get right all along, since the advent of e-books, it has been its predictions for the role of e-books, or digital versions of what had been printed books.

### What were some of the early, failed attempts at e-books?

Both Mike and Robert first got involved in what was then called "electronic publishing" in the early 1990s as co-organizers of the first conferences that discussed digital change across publishing, including trade publishing. In the early 1990s, there were no smartphones and the hand-held personal digital assistants were primitive. When we thought about delivering books to people as digital files, we thought about PDFs or .doc files that would almost certainly be "read" on a desktop PC, because even laptop computers were then still relatively rare.

At the time, we also shared a client that had an idea for a digital book with a twist. The notion was to combine paged text that looked like a book (a very forward-thinking idea at the time) with spreadsheet and computation functionality built in. The client's "book" on retirement included a calculating capability managing a questionnaire that addresses "How much do I need to save each month from now on to have enough when I'll want to retire?"

These e-books, which had design that included simulated "page-turning," were very lightweight (didn't require a lot of code) and were delivered on floppy disks (which by this time weren't actually "floppy"; they were rigid, but they had retained the name). Everybody's computers had floppy disk drives.

But, unfortunately for our client, at that very moment (about 1994), Microsoft had persuaded just about every computer manufacturer on the planet to put CD-ROM drives into their computers as well. Microsoft had a very legitimate commercial incentive to promote this technology. Computer code that might require ten or eighteen floppy disks could all be squeezed on one CD-ROM. That sharply cut Microsoft's cost of goods for the about-to-deliver Windows95, the Microsoft operating system that used graphics for the first time and enabled Windows to really compete with Apple.

With Microsoft pushing the CD-ROM concept, the conventional wisdom at the time was that products delivered on floppy disks, with so much less "richness" than what a CD-ROM would hold, wouldn't be competitive in the new razzle-dazzle marketplace of products that CD-ROM drives in every computer would create.

And thus began a wild goose chase that lasted over a decade, as many publishers proceeded on the tacit assumption that "just the text" for a digital book wasn't enough and that they had to invent something better than a book. Of course, "better" meant using more computer capability, so experiments were expensive, requiring sound, video, complex graphics, and all sorts of other things that had nothing to do with reading a book. And they also had nothing to do with the content that book publishers had the expertise to develop.

Our client at the time got nowhere. They were raising money from the tech world, so their funding sources wouldn't allow them to accept our advice to stick with their original idea on floppy disks. They absolutely had to make CD-ROM products. So they spent a lot more money gussying up their offering, adding no value to their very useful original idea, and ultimately delivering a product in a format that only a small minority of the computers in use could actually handle. (It takes a long time to turn over the installed base and they were, unfortunately, delivering a CD-ROM product at such an early stage that the CD-ROM installed base was pretty minimal.)

### How did the formats evolve for simple e-books?

People who believed in simple e-books—just the text delivered to a computer screen instead of a printed page—were pretty rare in the late 1990s. Two start-ups developed to deliver e-books on small proprietary hand-held devices: Rocketbook and Softbook. The former was smaller and really worked only for text; the latter was a larger screen format and was intended to be able to handle some simple graphics, which made it at least functional for books that required any graphics or illustrations. The two companies were acquired by Gemstar before they hit the marketplace. They got nowhere.

Then two formats developed to compete with PDFs and .doc files but for display on existing devices, attacking the challenge of "reflowing" the text onto different-sized screens. One was invented by Microsoft and was called MS Reader. The other was invented by an upstart called Peanut Press, who very smartly made an e-reader software to display books on the Palm Pilot. Palm was by far the leading "personal digital assistant," handheld devices used primarily as appointment diaries and address books.

Of course, Peanut Press was all about selling the e-books, so they had zero interest in passing the sales along to established online book retailers. When Palm itself acquired Peanut, they followed the model of keeping the sales to themselves. Microsoft, perhaps recalling the success they'd had making their operating system work across computers while Apple had hardware and software combined in one package, wanted MS Reader compatible with multiple devices and available through as many resellers as possible.

They had different business models. Palm decided to sell their Palm Digital Books themselves through their own website. Microsoft was inclined to allow MS Reader to be sold by other resellers. Along with MS Reader, Microsoft also introduced the PocketPC, a handheld device intended to compete with the Palm Pilot. It never gained serious traction.

All of this device and format proliferation made it very difficult for either of the two online book retailers—Amazon and BN.com—to play in the e-book space. Palm's strategy effectively shut them out completely, MS Reader never had enough devices to build much of a market, and the PDF format—which worked on all desktop and laptop computers—never gained consumer acceptance as a viable way to read a book.

Then along came a new proprietary format called Mobi, which for a moment seemed poised to cut the Gordian knot. The Mobi format would work within either MS Reader or Palm! With Mobi, a single file could be sold to satisfy the small group of e-book readers (which included author Mike Shatzkin, who started reading books on his Palm Pilot regularly from the moment the opportunity presented itself), regardless of their desired format.

In 2005, before the proposition could be tested that Mobi would enable a real e-book market to develop because one format would suit multiple devices, Amazon bought Mobi—which later became the spine of the Kindle format—and took it off the market. Shortly thereafter, neither Amazon nor BN.com was selling e-books.

In 2004, Sony, which had experimented with e-books for years, essentially revived the Rocket and Softbooks model of a dedicated e-reading device and offered the Sony Reader hardware and e-book format. This proved to be as unsuccessful commercially as the gussied-up files the CD-ROMs had coaxed publishers to make. Trying to force e-book readers to buy and use a dedicated device looked at the time like a very difficult proposition.

### How did the reading public come around to reading books on screens?

Reading on a screen was an idea people had to get used to. Forcing them to buy a device dedicated to something they weren't sure they wanted to do—and compounded by the fact that so few of the most commercial books were available in digital format (because why would publishers spend money to digitize for such a small audience?)— seemed like a very hard way to get people to substitute screens for paper for their book reading. Palm continued to be the leading e-book format because Palm devices were ubiquitous, but nobody bought one to use it as an e-book reader. They used it as an e-book reader because they already owned it.

### How did Amazon shape e-books?

In November 2007, Amazon launched the Kindle. That was a dedicated device primarily for e-book reading, although it ostensibly could also process email and do very slow, unsatisfying, and monochrome web browsing.

But Amazon tackled and solved a number of problems that nobody else had really acknowledged.

First, they used their clout with publishers to get most of the newest and best books made available in the format, which they hadn't been before. Palm, Microsoft, and Sony all really had to introduce themselves to book publishers. By the time of the Kindle, however, Amazon had been a growing account for every publisher for over a decade.

Second, they enabled connecting the device directly to the content, and, at first, before there was Wi-Fi for connecting, Amazon enabled and *paid for* the dial-up connections that getting to the internet required. Palm had required downloading to a computer and then synching the computer that had taken in the files to the handheld device. The dedicated Sony reader didn't have connectivity; you put books into it by synching to a regular PC.

Third, Amazon was able to put the e-book offerings right into the stream of book commerce, since most of the online book sales went through them. Amazon had the ability to say "Would you like it as an e-book?" directly to a person searching for a particular title.

### How did Amazon's kindle release change e-book sales?

The initial price for a Kindle was $400, perhaps set high to help cover the risk Amazon took that the dial-ups they were paying for might be used to shop and not buy. Or worse, the Kindle owner might even use that precious dial-up time to look at web pages on their hobbled and monochrome device. So you'd have to be a pretty serious reader to buy one. That meant the device price effectively screened out light users, so, even before Amazon used their most powerful weapon—pricing—Kindle owners were self-selected as the group of readers who would buy e-books in volumes highly disproportionate to their numbers.

But what turned into the most brilliant part of the rollout strategy was Amazon's reversal of the time-honored "razors and blades" strategy. Gillette and Schick had learned long ago to sell razors cheaply to lock in customers who would then provide lots of profits buying replacement blades. They'd almost give the razors away to assure themselves a stream of blades business.

Amazon stood this on its head.

Perhaps to make the device prices palatable, but perhaps with bigger strategic thoughts in mind, Amazon sold Kindle e-books at a sharp discount from established publisher prices for paper books. This had never been the practice before. Palm, MS Reader, and Sony e-books had all taken every bit of the margin the publisher price gave them. (After all, they were building out expensive delivery technology to be in the e-book business at all!) But Amazon, buying e-books as the others did at 50 percent off the publisher-suggested price for a regular book, cut the price considerably for their consumers. They were even willing to cut it below their cost for some titles.

This made the overall commercial equation—reader device plus cost of content—look attractive to heavy book consumers. If you read three books a year, the Kindle ecosystem was very expensive. But if you read three books a *week*, the device cost melted away from the savings on the individual e-book purchases.

Before long, the Kindle e-book volumes were not only getting publishers' attention but were also noticed by Barnes & Noble. At first B&N developed Nook as a reading system option designed to work on other hardware (but not on the Kindle e-reader). Pretty quickly thereafter, B&N developed Nook as their competitor to the Kindle device.

### How did the other dedicated e-readers and the multipurpose devices change e-books?

When the iPhone began the smartphone revolution in 2008 and tablets also started to become ubiquitous, Google and the Canadian upstart e-book system called Kobo entered the fray as well. Both created software that enabled use of their reading systems on many devices. Kobo offered devices competitive to Kindles and Nooks as well.

Over the first two years of Kindle's existence, publishers could see these competitors trying to enter the market but being starved for oxygen by Amazon's e-book pricing strategy. Although Amazon always maintained that its overall e-book business yielded a positive margin, they were selling many high-profile e-books for less than the price they were paying publishers for them in order to meet their own internal mandate to keep e-book prices at $9.99 and below.

In this environment, e-book sales started to soar. Amazon, Barnes & Noble, Kobo, and Google were all really pushing e-book sales. Amazon, B&N, and Kobo were all committed to dedicated reading devices, for which the prices kept dropping. Meanwhile, Amazon was opening up its system to independent authors, who were undercutting even Amazon's aggressive pricing. More and more e-books came into the market from them at prices that were almost trivial, ranging from 99 cents to a few bucks. These independent authors didn't have printed versions that cost more to "protect" and many of them valued getting readers more than dollars.

In addition, e-books enabled something print couldn't do because of physical constraints: making a chunk of a book available as a free sample. Over time, the amount of content available for nothing or very little became a powerful magnet to encourage people with a device that could read the sample to try e-books.

Publishers saw a real threat to their businesses. E-book sales were rising steadily at prices print books couldn't come near. Amazon had already disrupted the print market quite a bit with its discounting; now it threatened to upend the whole book market with cheap e-books as well. Although e-book sales were still a small percentage of the total, publishers thought they saw handwriting on the wall saying very scary things.

### What is the agency model of e-book pricing and how did it come about?

In the history of e-books, there is "before Apple" and "after Apple"; that company represents the last big disruptive entrant to the e-book market.

The iPhone came out in June of 2008. In March of 2009, Kindle created an iOS app that enabled Kindle to be read on the iPhone. The other formats quickly followed. With the iPad, the new tablet computer format, scheduled to hit the market in early 2010, Apple saw itself well positioned to deliver a superior e-reading experience, particularly for books that went beyond the words-on-a-flat-surface formula that was, so far, the only thing that really worked for e-books.

So it made sense for Apple to create its own e-book format, iBooks, and to sell them in its own iBookstore. By the fall of 2009, Apple was planning its new initiative to launch in April 2010, right behind the release of the iPad.

And publishers saw here an opportunity to rewrite the commercial rules of the e-book market. They saw a chance to kill two birds with one stone. They could reduce the "just like print" model of giving half the retail price to the supply chain. And, at the same time, they could stop the discounting of e-books that they believed seriously threatened their core business of selling print books through brick-and-mortar retailers.

These two objectives would be achieved by the introduction of "agency pricing." The idea was that the retailers didn't actually "sell" the books; the "publishers" did through the retailers acting as their "agents." Since publishers were selling the books, they set the price. To be fair, the price to the consumer would be the same from all retailers. And, at the same time, the retailer would be rewarded with 30 percent of the consumer price.

How did the implementation of agency pricing go? Apple was more than willing to sign on to those terms, which relieved them of the requirement to manage price variation as a marketing element. They negotiated maximum prices for e-books that were lower than but pegged to the prevailing print prices. Of course, some of the price-lowering was offset for the publishers because the agency model delivered them 70 percent of the price that was set rather than 50 percent. Publishers did all they could to make what ended up being a joint action by five large houses look like a set of individual decisions. (There were six big houses at the time: Penguin, HarperCollins, Hachette, Macmillan, and Simon & Schuster switched to agency; Random House stayed out at first.)

And Apple was more than happy with the new protocol. Thirty percent matched their notion of what the system owner should get on a sale within the system. The agency model relieved it of the need to think about individual title pricing, a skill that competitors Amazon and B&N had years of experience developing and Apple did not.

So in April 2010, the iBookstore opened and the new agency model began. E-books from the five agency publishers were sold at the new prices, usually higher than the $9.99 Amazon had tried to establish as the e-book maximum.

Random House's absence from iBookstore was calculated. They figured that with the other big houses now requiring agency price uniformity, Amazon would happily discount and feature their books very heavily. They were right. And they figured all along that if the iBookstore suddenly took off and they were losing too much by not being there, they could correct the error and join up later.

As it happened, the biggest publisher successfully gamed the system. Indeed, with apps already in place in the iOS system for the competing formats, iBookstore did not devastate other e-book retailers, even for sales within the rapidly growing iPhone and iPad installed bases.

But after a year, Random House switched strategies again, and in March 2011, they announced they were moving to agency pricing and making their e-books available through iBookstore. But they won twice with their delay. When they made the change, a senior executive told author Mike Shatzkin explicitly that the motivation was to enable independent stores that were hoping to sell e-books through Kobo or Google to compete for those sales. They couldn't do that if Amazon was continuing to steeply discount Random House books. Random House effectively said that their dedication to maintaining a strong independent store network trumped short-term sales and profit gains.

The first indication that their strategy was a success was that their sales in the year they were holdouts got a huge boost from Amazon discounting while, at the same time, they were collecting payments based on the much higher retail prices they had always set. (Although they only got 50 percent, not 70 percent, they still usually came out ahead on each unit.)

The second time Random House won was a year later when in March 2012 the US Department of Justice sued the five agency publishers for having colluded to raise consumer prices. Random House, having moved independently, was not included in the suit. So the publisher escaped the damages, primarily paid as discounts to consumers on future e-book sales, that the other publishers had to deal with.

### How did the agency pricing switch work for the big publishers?

Agency pricing has proven to be a decidedly mixed blessing for big publishers. The switch has effectively meant that the retailers have stopped giving any of their market share to cut consumer prices. (At first this was mandated by the rules of agency that publishers set; it continued that way after the government forced the publishers to "allow" some discounting.) The higher prices publishers charge for e-books have made it easier for independent authors and Amazon's own publishing programs to gain traction though price discounting, and the big publisher share of the e-book market appears to have steadily diminished since agency pricing began. Publishers take some comfort in the fact that print book sales have stabilized. It is not clear how much the lower e-book sales for the big houses are caused by the overall influx of e-books that come from outside the established base of suppliers: independent authors and new digital-first publishers.

There appear to be two enduring realities as we write in 2017. One is that fancy, gussied-up, multiple-function e-books have not established any audience appeal. The e-books that sell are of narrative writing, not more complex presentations, and they are just like the printed books but delivered digitally. They all have built-in dictionaries now and they are increasingly easy to navigate or take notes in. But perhaps the only facility that has taken hold beyond that is the combining of the audiobook and e-book so a "reader" can toggle between using her eyes and using her ears.

The other is that Amazon's share continues to grow. Kobo and Google have never gained much traction in the US and UK markets. Nook had initial success when it captured e-book readers from the ranks of store customers who had not been exposed to the first wave of Kindle marketing through Amazon, but their share—like Kobo's and Google's—appears to continue to slide. The most robust competitor to Kindle is iBooks, but it seems to gain share at the expense of the others while Kindle just continues to grow.

# 6

# THE BOOK PUBLISHING BUSINESS MODEL

## *How do trade publishers make money?*

Take, as an almost absurd example of this business model, the companies that merged in 2013 to become Penguin Random House (PRH)—in 2016 they are said by *Publishers Weekly* to have had €3.7 billion in revenues, on the backs of 15,000 new titles worldwide. Let's assume that their backlist is three times as large as the frontlist, so real annual revenues per title across a universe of about 60,000 titles would be €80,000 per title per year. Add to that the subsidiary formats each title is published in and you have a roughly €4 billion enterprise whose revenues are delivered each year from a newly constituted mix of over 100,000 front- and backlist ISBNS.

In the earlier chapters we laid out the amount of work that goes into acquiring, marketing, and selling a single title; the apparatus required to successfully publish this volume of titles is enormous. So it is perhaps no surprise that according to *Publishers Weekly*, PRH has 12,500 employees worldwide.

This workforce is divided into employees who work directly for a given house or imprint, and thus work on the sliver of the total output of titles that come from that business unit—usually in either editorial or marketing—and those whose who are responsible for a whole division's title output (e.g., sales), or for the overall company (e.g., finance).

On the other end of the pipeline there are thousands of accounts making up the market for a publisher's titles who are selling those books to literally millions of individual readers. Even with the phenomenal consolidation of sales in Amazon, the wholesalers, and B&N, even a mid-sized publisher is faced with selling several thousand titles in a variety of formats to at least 5,000 accounts.

The sheer diffusion of the underlying numbers in publishing, on both the product and account side, might suggest to some an unstable business model. Aside from a few key titles on the product side that are new each year, the ballast of the backlist and the sheer number of "bets" a publisher makes each year instead actually deliver remarkable stability in most publishers' financial results. It appears remarkable from the outside, perhaps, but this variety show, this mix of the brand-new author, a new subject matter, or the new category that inevitably appears every few years (sodoku books, adult coloring books, or even the crossword puzzle books that were integral to the success of Simon & Schuster in its start-up years) is what keeps publishing vibrant.

And although every new book is an entirely new product, the very low cost of introducing one additional title into the mix allows a publisher to try new authors, subjects, and formats very cheaply. In fact, many of a house's biggest successes still come from "sleeper" titles whose huge sales potential isn't recognized by the publisher until the book is actually on sale in the marketplace.

### How are publishing companies built, and then rebuilt each year from ever-changing titles?

Publishing companies get from one year to the next, even with the variable success that depends on what books they have published season by season, by organizing the editorial or product development aspects of the business into small operating units.

For all the consolidation of ownership in publishing, the internal organization of staff and title output on the editorial, marketing, and publicity sides of the business is still by house or imprint or by "brand." Some of these smaller units are rolled up into "divisions" inside the corporate umbrella. The extreme case is PRH which is divided worldwide into 250 imprint brands. And each of these "brands" is an "operating unit" each with its own "budget" and target for revenue and spending control.

The impact of this structure is to reproduce the focus and sense of mission of a small to medium-sized publishing company inside a consolidated corporate giant. This works more effectively at some companies than others, and in fact is often heavily influenced by how the personalities mesh within a particular organization. Each company has its own rules about the independence and freedom of decision-making allowed each operating unit.

### What does the math of title acquisition look like?

From the beginning of time as far as we can see, publishers have been most comfortable viewing each title as an individual profit center, as we discussed in Chapter 2, explaining the utility of a P&L at the acquisitions stage. It is usually easy enough to recognize the revenue attributable to a particular title and, of course, the direct costs of the author advance or royalty, the typesetting and page makeup, and the printing and binding on a title-by-title basis. But the per-title cost of lots of other elements is not so clear, from the editors' or marketers' time on a title to the sales and warehousing expenses and rent: these are instead part of the house's overhead costs.

To judge the relative success or failure of a given title, by a given author, brought in by a given editor, a post-mortem is prepared by the finance group perhaps two years after publication and is reviewed by the publisher and editor. Perhaps to put this review in context—or perhaps to guide the acquisition decisions when they're made—the initial acquisition P&L is structured in the same way, with as many direct expenses and projected sales as possible matched and directly attributed to a particular title.

The acquisition P&L typically pushes down allocations of division and corporate overheads in the form of percentages of net sales to reflect the "costs." That affects the hurdle that each new title must exceed in order to meet the financial criteria for acquisition.

The truth is that this method of calculating costs is a fiction: each book published does not actually result in an increase in overhead of anything like the standard percentage, if it results in any increase in overhead at all! So the standard calculation actually forces the new title to perform better than it would actually need to do to add to the house's profits.

When publishers decide whether or not to buy a book, or they look back at a book to evaluate its performance, the analysis is done in a way that could be, and often is, misleading. This is almost universal practice, has been for at least a century, and may never change. But it is worth a few minutes for anybody interested in understanding the profitability of a publishing house to contemplate what seems to us to be rampant misunderstanding.

The problem is that the practice of constructing P&Ls on a book-by-book basis is itself a logical fallacy. The idea of an individual book making a profit or loss makes sense only if there is no publishing house. That is, if you decide this afternoon to take time off from your career as a truck driver or a banker and invest a little cash in publishing a book, your exercise could at some point be measured and a profit or loss could be calculated.

Doing that would be very straightforward if you were doing it on a cash basis. You'd add up all the revenue you got from publishing the book and all the expenses you incurred in publishing it and pursuing that revenue, mash them together, and have your calculated profit or loss. You would have to account for unsold inventory if you didn't use a print-on-demand strategy. You might have net positive cash (profit) or net negative cash (loss) and some unsold inventory (potential additional profit) that you might have to pay storage fees on (potential additional loss).

Standard accrual accounting methods would call that unsold inventory an "asset," essentially adding to your "profit," but that would be true only if you could actually sell it.

If you had to hire a designer for your book or a production manager to help you get it printed, those costs would have been included in what you deducted. If you paid commissions to a sales force or hired a marketer to help you, those costs also would be transparent and in the calculations.

But if you decided to grow your little operation and do ten books, even on a cash basis the accounting for each book now wouldn't be quite as simple. Your production or marketing or sales team would now work on your whole list, and the amount of their time that should be "allocated" to each book might be hard or even impossible to calculate. If you were being precise about it, you'd have to account for the reality that the books are not all the same. They take different amounts of effort to develop editorially and do not place consistent demands on your production and distribution overhead costs. You couldn't actually just "add up" all the expenses for each book to subtract from the revenues to produce a profit calculation.

And imagine how much harder it would be to be precise about assigning those costs if you were dealing with hundreds of books in an organization each year. Or thousands.

Because many publishing decisions are made one book at a time and because accounting is done to the government to pay taxes and (sometimes) to shareholders as well, it is common to do the accounting on a per-title basis and ultimately on a per-unit basis (where we aren't just trying to understand the profit—or loss—by title, but are attempting literally to score things down to the individual unit transacted).

Title P&Ls and unit cost accounting are part of the operating fabric of every large publishing house and both are structurally unsound ways to think about the enterprise. Publishing would work better if they weren't standard procedures. To the extent they are needed to pay taxes or report financials, of course they should be calculated and used. But they are very bad guides for making operating decisions despite the fact that they are almost universally employed.

### How do publishers calculate their profits?

Here's how book-publishing economics actually works. A publishing house has overheads that are reasonably fixed: primarily rent and salaries but also travel and entertainment, insurances, legal and accounting, and the costs all businesses have to keep operating and keep their doors open. Unless there is some conscious expansion or contraction of the publishing program, those expenses do not fluctuate appreciably based on the number of titles a house publishes or the revenues it generates from selling books and rights.

Then each book has two kinds of costs: the investments required to publish it at all (author's advance and what used to be called design and typesetting but which would now be better described as "creating a print-ready file") and unit production costs, the "paper, presswork, and binding" of the actual printed units. There is virtually no incremental unit cost for each additional e-book, even though there are real costs getting e-books "set up" that are separate from getting the print version ready for press.

When books or rights sell, the publisher banks a "margin." For rights, that is all the revenue not paid through to the author. For book sales, it is "contribution margin," the difference between what revenue the publisher receives from accounts and the actual direct costs required to complete the sale, which for most books requires subtracting the unit printing cost and any incremental sales commission and royalty due to the author (if the advance has earned out). The margin earned on each book has to "pay back" the book's direct investments first but then gets applied to address overhead.

When the net positive margin generated by all the books, frontlist and backlist, in a fiscal year have covered the house's overhead, the additional margin constitutes the house's profit. One might say the book's "profit" is the margin generated, but no publishing house we know looks at it that way.

Instead, the standard practice is to assign each book its "share" of the house's overheads. (Sometimes this is made even more complicated by assigning different overheads to books from different reporting units—imprints—within the house.) The method for calculating the number to apply in each house is not transparent, and almost certainly these methods vary, but the simplest form would be for the house to calculate what the fixed overheads were last year in relation to total sales and "allocate" each book that percentage of overheads. (The overhead number often ends up being 35 to 45 percent.) That overhead allocation pushes many, if not most, books from being calculated as "profitable" to being shown as "unprofitable."

### What might be a better way of calculating the profits of publishing?

A more precise statement of the reality of this math is that a few books generate margins in excess of the house's overall overheads percentage and many, if not most, do not.

Here's why this matters. It makes a house see specific titles as "unprofitable," even though the financial results of publishing them are actually indispensable to the profits of the house. Let's unpack that a bit.

Mike's father, Leonard Shatzkin, the person who long ago laid out this framework for publishing economics, suggested that every house that believes in assigning a percentage for "overhead" to the calculation of title profitability do the following exercise. Recalculate last year's business but throw out—pretend you didn't publish—all the books this overhead-inclusive analysis would call "unprofitable." You lose all the direct revenues and you lose all the direct costs. And then you recalculate your overall performance.

What would have happened? You would have lost your shirt! Why? Because all the books that earned 3 percent or 8 percent or 20 percent, but not the stipulated average percentage, actually contributed dollars of margin that paid your rent and other fixed costs. You take those out and you're running your company with not enough volume or margin.

There is more than one logical fallacy at work here, but here's the big one: it is a mistake to require the minimum overhead contribution to equal the house's average overhead contribution in order to deem a particular book "profitable." In fact, if you think about that for even a couple of minutes, it seems nuts.

Mike's father's insight did stick with and inspire one very successful CEO, Tom McCormack. McCormack was an editor at Doubleday when Leonard Shatzkin was there in the 1950s inventing Dolphin Books, one of the first trade paperback imprints in a major hardcover house. McCormack landed the CEO-ship of St. Martin's in 1969. Over the next three decades, McCormack built a publishing powerhouse that is now the backbone of Macmillan.

McCormack is quite certain that the practice of measuring a book's potential "contribution," rather than creating an artificial P&L that incorporated an overhead percentage, was a primary driver of St. Martin's period of profitable title growth. And the title growth was the primary driver of the company's revenues and earnings growth, which was continuous, substantial, and has resulted in Macmillan being one of the Big Five publishers today.

Of course, things have changed a lot since Len Shatzkin formulated these ideas and even since Tom McCormack executed them. Before the rise of indie publishing enabled by Amazon, it was much easier for the big houses with their big sales and distribution capabilities to be sure they'd get thousands of copies out on just about every book they did. Now it happens—and it really didn't back then—that even a big house can have frequent abject failures: books that don't even recover their direct costs (even without a massive advance against royalties). That was a much rarer event in bygone decades.

But that's a separate problem. No major house takes on a project thinking they'll get only a few hundred copies out.

That book would fail anybody's profitability test. But the question houses should be asking is whether the way they model titles in advance might actually be stopping them from publishing books that would have improved their profitability, even with the sales estimates they're working with.

### What are the practical implications of the consolidations and mergers that have occurred in publishing?

The biggest impact of any given merger is on costs. Savings on manufacturing, combining sales forces, consolidating warehousing, eliminating duplicated editorial and marketing expenses, and general shaving of general overheads might net the surviving entity between 3 and 5 percentage points on the P&L. To increase your bottom line by 25 percent is significant, especially if the savings are baked into your margin going forward.

The second, which is related, is on the negotiating leverage that comes with size. In a world where Amazon accounts for sales of over 50 percent of a publisher's print book sales and an even greater percentage of their e-book volume, a publisher like Penguin Random has a much better chance of holding its own at the negotiating table with Amazon when setting terms. More important, perhaps they can use their clout from volume to get the best placement, marketing programs, and just plain attention for their titles (from Amazon and from everybody else).

Interestingly, the size of a company—even a massive change in size, for example, after a merger of two large companies—does not have an impact on revenues. Once the acquisition of another house is made and the various editorial groups are examined in detail, the actual title output and revenues might dip slightly from the sum of the two companies before the merger.

And while sheer size may allow the combined house to pay more for some authors or attract some who want to be part of this new publishing Olympus, others have been known to seek what is perceived to be the more intimate and dedicated treatment that an imprint at a mid-sized company can give them. Most of the advantages of size are available to authors published by companies ranked below the very top tier, say from no. 6 to no. 20.

# 7

# BOOKSELLING IN THE TWENTY-FIRST CENTURY— AMAZON.COM

*How has Amazon influenced publishing?*

Although Amazon began identifying itself as "earth's biggest bookstore" and pretty much only sold books for the first few years of its existence, it has clearly outgrown its roots. Nevertheless, for obvious reasons given our focus in this book, we are going to take a publishing-centric view of the company in this chapter. Amazon has, in fact, outgrown the industry of its origin. Our analysis of Amazon today—its commercial ambitions, its economic health, its role in the world—makes us believe that bookselling and publishing almost certainly constitute less than 10 percent of the company's total revenues and far less than 10 percent of its gross margin.

But while books and publishing may be tertiary activities in Amazon's world, Amazon's activities are increasingly dominating publishing's world. It is hard to be precise in measuring this, but Amazon's sales of print books today appear to us to exceed half the print books sold in the United States, and their share continues to grow here and around the world.

In addition, Amazon's Kindle format dominates the global e-book market and operates the (to date) *only* commercially significant e-book subscription service. With commercial publishers allowing (some might say "encouraging") diminishing sales in that format with pricing strategies calculated to boost print, the sales oxygen will become increasingly scarce for Amazon's e-book competitors.

As we write, Amazon is also moving aggressively to build a brick-and-mortar store capability, the future shape of which is still unknown. But since Barnes & Noble is candid about shrinking its bookselling presence, mass merchants are finding books less attractive than they used to be, and independent bookstores are, at best, growing slowly, it seems like only a matter of time before Amazon is the leading seller of print online and offline as well as the dominant seller of e-books.

Combine that with the facts that Amazon (a) publishes books and (b) enables self-publishing by tens of thousands of authors, many of whom were previously working with established publishers, and you have a disruptive force that touches every corner of the book publishing industry.

The authors of this book were already book business veterans when Amazon was launched, and each had reason to follow Amazon from the beginning.

At the time of its emergence, Robert was a principal in a publishing consulting firm called Market Partners International (MPI). They were often hired by start-ups and others trying to introduce themselves to and navigate around the book business. In 1995, not long after Amazon opened, Jeff Bezos and his team engaged MPI. In that role, MPI worked with Amazon to make connections within the publishing industry, enabling the new company to better understand how the industry operated and how to get on publishers' radar as a serious new account. MPI organized a kickoff event for Amazon's participation in the 1997 BookExpo America (referred to in the industry as BEA) in Chicago that included Jeff Bezos speaking to the assembled publishers.

One of Robert's strongest memories of working with Bezos was a BEA conversation in which Robert repeatedly expressed surprise at the heavy discounting Amazon was doing on the site in the summer of 1998. Jeff was firm in his response that what mattered was building market share. Robert repeatedly countered with "price" and Jeff repeatedly answered with "market share" in a conversation that resembled a verbal ping-pong game, which in hindsight Robert admitted he lost.

### How can we quantify Amazon's growth in the book business in recent years?

This is an answer that conventional stats and analysis can't answer. Amazon is not totally transparent with their numbers. Fortunately, Data Guy—an industry sales data analyst discovered and popularized by indie author Hugh Howey, who has developed a unique way of tracking traditional and nontraditional trade book sales—has built a methodology to examine Amazon and industry numbers at a deeper level. So I asked the following two questions of Data Guy. After each question is Data Guy's reply.

### Can you explain the evolution of industry data discernment in the age of Amazon and indie publishing?

"Publishing industry data has always been an imperfect science. To measure overall industry activity, data providers obtain as much point-of-sale data as they can from the largest book retailers and publishers, under the assumption that those large publishers and retailers are responsible for the vast majority of book sales. They then project from that partial record of industry sales, combining it with statistics on the overall count of newly issued ISBN book identifiers during the period, to estimate the remaining portion of book sales—those which they can't see. With paper books, tracking the supply chain of total inventory that was printed, warehoused, shipped, and returned by distributors provided the industry with yet another gauge of overall activity that could be used to triangulate the unreported sales of smaller publishers.

"With the advent of digital books, which have no physical inventory to track through a supply chain, and which don't require ISBN numbers at all to sell through online book retailers like Amazon, Barnes & Noble, Apple, and Kobo, the previous industry methodology for estimating the unreported portion of all book sales completely broke down. Industry observers were left essentially blind to e-book and audiobook sales from smaller publishers and from self-published authors; analysts could only assume that, just as in print, their share of the market remained negligible or small.

"Between 2010 and 2014, however, that industry-wide assumption rapidly diverged from reality.

"Online book retailers such as Amazon, Barnes & Noble, Apple, and Kobo rolled out self-service digital publishing tools during this period, making it economically feasible for self-published authors to sell their books directly to a global audience, right alongside similar titles from large publishers. The low cost of digital publishing eliminated barriers to entry, leading to an explosion of digital-first or digital-only books from 'indie' self-published authors and other nontraditional publishers flooding into the market.

Sales of these untracked titles were not reported to any industry body; in fact, even a simple count of new titles released each year became impossible, as the vast majority of new digital books—including the highest selling ones—lacked traditional ISBN identifiers.

"By 2016, the industry's ability to track digital book sales had degenerated to the point where nearly two-thirds of consumer e-book purchases in the US weren't being counted in industry statistics. These traditional statistics weren't even directionally correct indicators of market trends anymore; journalists citing data from the AAP, Bookscan, and Pubtrack were reporting 'e-book sales declining industry-wide' year after year, at the same time online retailers were reporting overall e-book sales 'growing in both unit and dollar terms'—the difference being the now-hundreds of millions of annual e-book sales by self-published authors and other nontraditional providers that were going unreported.

"Closing this digital-sales tracking gap required borrowing a technique pioneered five years earlier in the video game industry—an industry which, like book publishing, had similarly seen a significant share of its sales migrate to new digital formats downloaded from online retailers, and away from physical media formats sold in stores.

"By web-scraping the millions of publicly available best-seller rankings and metadata which online retailers update hourly, and then calibrating against raw publisher-provided sales data for a subset of corresponding books, an overall picture of industry sales could again be derived with a fair amount of accuracy. At first unofficially, and then with increasing confidence in the validity of the numbers, publishers and industry analysts began turning to these web-scraping-based statistics to fill in the missing part of the industry sales puzzle."

*We know that Amazon book sales have continued to grow; to what extent is that growth expanding the market for established publishing and to what extent is it new business—indie authors and digital-first publishers—that might well never have existed in such numbers without Amazon's directed efforts to help and serve them?*

"Amazon's book sales have continued to grow by double-digit percentages, year after year, both in print formats (hardcovers and paperbacks) and in digital formats (e-books and downloadable audiobooks). On the print side, the source of Amazon's rapid growth splits roughly 50/50 between the zero-sum cannibalization of print sales drawn away from shrinking brick-and-mortar bookstores and actual expansion of the print-book market for established publishers, primarily due to Amazon's greater rural reach and steeper consumer discounting. On the digital side, for the last three or four years at least, Amazon's e-book sales growth has been almost entirely driven by lower-cost titles from self-published 'indie' authors, digital-first presses, and Amazon's own in-house publishing imprints. The more established publishers have seen very little of that e-book growth; the industry's largest publishers, by choosing to maintain higher e-book prices to avoid cannibalizing their print business, have actually seen their e-book sales shrink year over year since 2013."

### Why did Amazon start out in the book business?

The book business really was the very best place for what became known much later as "The Everything Store" to start. The vast number of potential books and the inability of any store to carry them all made books a great product category to showcase the advantages of online search and delivery. Not only that, there were already extant digital databases of the book industry's output, ready to be put online and made available for search.

In addition, there was little ambiguity about what a book actually *was*. Consumers could be comfortable buying books knowing their size and the number of pages and not feel they needed to see and touch them. In an attempt to get publishers to provide as many descriptive elements for their titles as possible, by 1998 Amazon was scoring publishers based on the completeness of their entries.

Later on, the "Look Inside" feature was invented so that Amazon and other online retailers could actually show the inside pages of the book to online customers. And the book's covers were always important to entice the online customer so that, over time, best practices in book cover design had to specifically address the online audience.

And on top of that, it was possible for the fledgling Amazon to get from a single source a very large percentage of the books they'd have orders for. In fact, there were two national wholesalers to choose from which both stocked a relatively high percentage of the available books: Ingram and Baker & Taylor. (Both companies still operate today.)

Bezos put himself, and thus his new company, in Seattle, within a few hours of a large Ingram warehouse and distribution center in Oregon, which at that time "mirrored" their main warehouse in Nashville, carrying inventory of just about any title Ingram kept in stock. Ingram would routinely get books to Bezos's garage in Seattle within a day of his ordering those books from them, if they were in stock. (If they weren't in stock, Ingram's systems would tell him that and, in turn, Bezos would flag that book for slower delivery and let the online customer know.)

All that meant that Amazon needed to stock *no inventory at all* to live up to their claim of being "Earth's biggest bookstore."

Another big advantage for Amazon in starting out with books was that the prices for them are set by the manufacturer and publicly announced. In the beginning, that gave Amazon customers confidence that the prices they were paying were reasonable and likely to be the same as what they'd see elsewhere. In time, that publisher-set price became a competitive weapon because Amazon's discounts against it enabled them to gain market share faster than they otherwise would have.

### How did Amazon build its initial directory of offerings?

What was interesting was that Bezos didn't acquire rights to post the Ingram database online; instead, he licensed the database from their rival, Baker & Taylor. B&T was more focused on library business at that time than Ingram, so they tended to carry more titles and have more titles in their database. But there were some chuckles about Amazon licensing it at the time because the B&T database had not been "cleaned" of out-of-print books. More than a decade had passed since its creation, so it had lots of books in it that were really no longer available.

But where some people saw a bug, Bezos saw a feature. He understood before others had thought it through that if people looked for a book and didn't find it at all, they'd assume "This store doesn't have it" and go shop elsewhere. But if people looked for a book, found it, and were told "It is out of print," they'd keep searching where they were and find a substitute.

### What innovations did Amazon bring to online retailing?

Perhaps the single most important early invention from Amazon was the "promise date" for delivery, or perhaps we should say the "*reliable* promise date." Bezos knew that if the book was in Ingram's Oregon warehouse, he'd get it and be able to ship it on to his customer in two days. If the book wasn't in Oregon but in a different Ingram warehouse or in a B&T warehouse, he could still calculate the time until he got it reliably. Then he moved on to sourcing from the publishers, which required more time and, as experience developed with different publishers, he could tell more precisely how much time he needed from different publishers.

Translating all this into dates for consumer expectation of delivery was not an exact science, but the promise dates were largely reliable. And they also managed consumer expectations, which reduced the need for expensive interaction with customers inquiring about order status. So a single innovation gave the customer a better experience, encouraged ordering that might not have otherwise taken place, and reduced Amazon's post-transaction expenses.

A second critical innovation by Amazon from the early days was creating affiliate relationships. This enabled any website to share in the revenues generated from book sales at Amazon if they sent Amazon the sale. That suddenly meant that authors, publishers, and other website owners whose pages created consumer interest in a book could share in the sale without having to get into the e-commerce business themselves. This rapidly gave Amazon a network of feeders that, in addition to the direct revenue they provided, increased their network of web connections and in turn boosted their "Google juice" and made Amazon appear higher in search engine rankings when consumers were looking for books.

Amazon came up with an attention-grabbing innovation: "one-click ordering." They patented and defended it, which quickly stopped Barnes & Noble from using it and have subsequently made millions licensing it. By storing a customer's critical data, including payment information, Amazon made it possible for customers to order online with one click. Legal action followed, but Amazon's patent rights to one-click ordering were sanctioned by the courts and expired only about two decades later in 2017. Other online sites, including Apple since the year 2000, have been paying Amazon for the right to use this pretty simple technology that Amazon had early staked a claim to.

Amazon's biggest differentiator is the Prime program, which gives free shipping and other perks to members who pay a fee for the benefits. So Amazon collects money for "nothing" (no particular product or service) in advance for a program which then encourages consumers to shift as much of their purchasing as possible to Amazon.

But perhaps Amazon's biggest innovative merchandising strategy was not about their own retailing at all. They quickly realized that anything they built for themselves could be rented to others. That first took the form of Amazon's "Marketplace," by which vendors of all kinds could use the Amazon platform to sell their goods through Amazon. The Marketplace enabled Amazon to scale rapidly as a vendor of things other than books. And that strategy is really the foundation of their "cloud computing" business, by which they sell computer storage and processing capacity to anybody. (This is an area in which Amazon competes with other internet behemoths, including Google and Microsoft.)

### Why weren't they copied more widely?

There had been a number of attempts at online bookselling before Amazon and at least one vendor, Undercover Book

Service, that attempted to sell you any book you wanted to buy through their 800 number: telephone ordering. (Undercover also sourced primarily from the wholesalers, but, obviously, could not offer the benefits of a searchable database by telephone.)

After it became clear what Amazon could do on Ingram's back—offering its customers reliable delivery of books without actually stocking any themselves—Ingram formally organized an effort to enable it for other booksellers, so any bookstore could compete with Amazon for online business. The new initiative was called I2S2 (I-squared, S-squared), for Ingram Internet Support Services.

From an external perspective, Amazon squashed the new idea before it could get off the ground by introducing deep discounting, taking most if not all of the profit out of online sales. That effectively killed any chance that indies en masse would catch on, build an online business leaning on Ingram, and threaten Amazon.

But a senior executive at Ingram, who was there at the time, recalls this as the start of Ingram's capability to drop-ship on behalf of its customers—which they call "third-party distribution"—a critical pillar of its business today. Indeed, drop-shipping and the ability to deliver print-on-demand are two capabilities Ingram developed at the time Amazon was starting that are fundamental elements of the global supply chain infrastructure that the rest of the industry can use to compete with Amazon. (And which Amazon makes use of as well to offer optimum service to its customers.)

### Why were Barnes & Noble and Borders weak competitors?

It is important to recall that it took quite some time for Amazon's book business to grow to a level that looked threatening to existing retailers or disruptive to the industry. B&N reacted early, creating a partnership in 1998 with the international publisher Bertelsmann (owners of Bantam Doubleday Dell in the United States, and shortly thereafter, of Random House as well) called Books Online (BOL). That was their early foray into online selling. In 2003, B&N bought out Bertelsmann's share and BN.com reverted to being a wholly owned B&N operation.

Borders, on the other hand, had no interest in online selling in the early days. (Or perhaps they had no stomach for the investment it required.) They formed a partnership with Amazon to handle online business in 2001.

The big bookselling chains failed to see either the disruption or mass volume potential of online bookselling, or, if they did, they failed to act.

BN.com always took a back seat to store sales, which is where the profits were for B&N (and also where the big costs were that needed throughput to support them). They wouldn't risk additional disruption of their core business by pricing competitively with Amazon. And until very recently (which was much too late), they made only the feeblest attempts to integrate the BN.com offering with the stores to make a unique service offering to their customers.

So both major US bookselling chains were really bystanders as Amazon grew from a fledgling effort in a garage in Seattle to being truly (not just rhetorically) the largest bookseller in the world.

### On which publishers did Amazon have the most impact early?

Amazon had a major impact on academic and professional publishers well before they were truly disruptive in trade. A client of Mike's, Cambridge University Press, told him in 2002 that Amazon had surpassed *all other US retail combined* at that point for their books. This tracked with what Mike was learning at that time doing work for Barnes & Noble: academic customers—that is, professors—had already largely turned to Amazon for their book purchasing.

### How did publishers' views of Amazon evolve?

This is an impossible question to answer with precision because there are a lot of publishers and many of them don't agree about Amazon to this day. So we report here our general impressions, built by personal contact with many players over time.

After Amazon's first couple of years, when it was clear that they were a real force and here to stay, many publishers saw them as a counterweight to the really dominant retailers, the Borders/Walden and B&N/Dalton chains. Over time, the general consensus evolved from one of hope to one with a large element of fear.

One thing that made big publishers take notice was Amazon's practice of negotiating individual contractual terms of sale with publishers rather than simply accepting "published terms." Part of this was driven by Amazon's unique needs: for reliable metadata and reliable fulfillment dates, for example.

But Amazon also created new opportunities, which created new issues. Early in the twenty-first century, they started their "Look Inside" feature, which enabled their customers to replicate the in-store experience of looking at a book's pages to inform the purchase decision. One publisher has told us that a very prominent author suddenly saw chunks of his book content showing up on Amazon's search engine (A9, which once upon a time Amazon might have hoped would compete with Google). Amazon had taken the scans intended for "Look Inside" and used them for another purpose that had them displayed as online content found through search rather than by shopping at their site.

In time it evolved that having the whole book content was as valuable for Amazon in producing better search results as it was for Google (which had its own scanning programs at the same time). Better search results improved the book's sales, so that better sales, rather than the consumer browsing element, became the argument Amazon put forth to convince publishers to put books into the program.

But as Amazon grew, so did their demands in the contractual negotiations with publishers. Amazon knew they were most publishers' most profitable account: high volume, bulk shipments, very low returns, and sales across the entire breadth of a publisher's list. It was natural for them to figure out ways to claw back margin, through higher discounts, marketing programs, and fees. And as their sales continued to grow, this became more and more concerning to publishers. So when Amazon first entered the e-book business, then dominated it very early, warning lights flashed at nearly every publisher.

### How did Amazon kick-start the e-book business?

One tenet of Amazon's merchandising philosophy from the very beginning was that they wanted the maximum possible variety of offerings, expressed both as numbers of titles *and* as numbers of formats for each title. That core belief stood them in very good stead when they decided to get into the e-book business with Kindle, which launched in November 2007.

With the benefit of hindsight, we can identify at least four substantial differences between Amazon's approach to e-books and the prior efforts from tech giants Palm,

Microsoft, and Sony and a whole slew of start-ups that had tried to make what seemed like an obvious business work for over a decade without very much success.

First, Amazon made their Kindle device connect directly to content, which loaded into it without needing to go through a personal computer first. This massively simplified content acquisition for the consumer although it entailed a risk to Amazon. These were the days before ubiquitous Wi-Fi and the company could provide connectivity only by contracting to pay for dial-up from the device. If consumers had used that connectivity for purposes *other than* buying new e-books (from downloading free samples to using the crude-and-slow-but-available ability to use the Kindle for email or web browsing) this could have been a very costly feature for Amazon to provide.

Second, Amazon used its clout with publishers (and its own ability to finance conversions) to produce a huge increase in available titles, and particularly *desirable* titles. Amazon persuaded many publishers to make e-books available when the printed book first came out at a time when publishers were experimenting with and inclined to a "windowing" strategy: holding back the e-book's initial release the way they did the paperbacks and, usually, the audio version. (Delaying audio had a practical component; the separate production took time and couldn't begin in any case until the book manuscript was complete. Of course, the way publishers made e-books back then was also to work from the finished printing files, but the conversion process to an e-book file was much less demanding than the whole production needed to deliver audio.)

Third, Amazon's pricing strategy for the device and content reversed the normal razors and blades approach, which we discussed in Chapter 5. Shaving equipment manufacturers made their razors "cheap" so you'd be hooked on their "format" and made their money selling the compatible blades. Amazon made the initial Kindle device quite expensive ($400) but made the ecosystem attractive by selling the e-books themselves for a maximum price of $9.99. That meant that the whole deal was most commercially attractive to the heaviest readers. But, like the connectivity commitment, it came with financial risk. The $9.99 price Amazon wanted to establish as a maximum was more than their cost basis for many e-books at the time. In the short run, the profit on device sales probably covered them. In the longer run, Amazon almost certainly assumed that they'd get the marketplace clout to force publishers to lower their prices sufficiently to make Amazon's e-book revenues profitable as they became increasingly substantial.

(For whatever it is worth, Amazon has always claimed that they made positive margin on actual e-book sales overall, even in the days they were discounting many bestsellers as loss-leaders.)

And fourth, Amazon had the regular attention of almost every online book purchaser. No other online retailer of books, including BN.com, had as much as a tenth of Amazon's market share when the Kindle was introduced. So Amazon's repeated promotion of the Kindle and the practice of reading e-books was hammered home to the core audience from the first moment.

### How did Amazon really originate the self-publishing business?

Long before the development of the Kindle, Amazon had bought a print-on-demand company called Book Surge. Book Surge was a competitor to Ingram's Lightning Print for printing single copies, but they took a different approach. Ingram built a centralized print-and-bind facility (which grew into several locations over time). Book Surge had contracted with printers around the world to deliver their printed books. It was a network that agreed to a standard. As such, it had less "capability" (to deliver various trim sizes, for example) but the potential advantage of printing closer to the point of need. And that approach saved Amazon a lot of equipment and operations investment that would have been needed to ensure enough business to avoid those costs becoming a millstone.

Amazon turned Book Surge into CreateSpace, their own branded ability to deliver single copies.

Although they apparently were never jointly marketed to indie authors with a ribbon tied around them, the combination of Kindle and CreateSpace enabled a self-publishing revolution. It took only a year or so before there were enough Kindle reading devices in place—shortly thereafter the growth accelerated by apps for iPhones (and, of course, other e-book formats)—so that "self-publishing" through Amazon became the first commercially viable vanity publishing capability.

Soon authors discovered that they could be effective going directly to the public. Fledgling authors used Kindle that way with very inexpensive e-books (99 cents and up) that caught the Kindle readers' attention because of price. They were joined by authors who had reclaimed their backlists from publishers. When it became the case that an author could reach the entire Amazon universe with print and e-books and another adjacent e-book audience that was cumulatively half the size of Kindle through their e-book competitors Nook, Kobo, and Google, the indie title base started to mushroom.

Since by far the biggest part of that audience was reached through the one-stop shop at Amazon, many indies saw no need to go any further. While the most ambitious indie authors would set up with other e-book houses or with the service provider Ingram—which could get their content *everywhere* through e-books or print—the net result was that Amazon and Kindle continued to build their lead in available titles, a trend that continues to this day.

### How did Amazon change the used book market?

Once Amazon had facilitated their "Marketplace," enabling other retailers to use their customers and billing and collection capability, it was a short step to enable customers to sell as used books the books they'd bought previously, when they were finished with them.

Regardless of Amazon, the used book business was going to be disrupted by the internet. Prices in the used book market were kept high by effective scarcity. You'd go to a used bookstore and browse looking for things you wanted with no knowledge at all if the "gem" you found was one-on-the-planet or available at every used bookstore within a day's drive.

Suddenly, online databases could make all used books everywhere available anywhere. That challenged the core model of the business and drove prices down. When Amazon started to enable customers to resell their books *and* started offering used copies of books on the same product pages where it sold new books (because the margins weren't that different to Amazon and making all the choices available was the best thing for their customers), they fundamentally changed the role of used books in the marketplace.

Suddenly, every bestseller had competition with the copies of the same book that had sold last week or last month. The more copies it sold, the more used books could follow it into the marketplace. That meant that all the books—including books newly on the bestseller list—had used copies available at a substantial discount from the new book price. So it got structurally harder for publishers to sustain bestsellerdom. If there was a silver lining here, it was that purchasers of new books who wanted to do a little work could get some of their money back selling them through Amazon, which might make them more willing to spring for a new book.

This is a black box to publishers and authors. They really have no idea at all how many copies Amazon sells of current titles, or when they sell them, or for how much. Once, in 2005, a used book study was done that Amazon participated in. The estimates from that study were that only 16 percent of Amazon's used book sales impinged on the sales of new books. Without any examination of how that calculation was done at the time, it would seem a fair assumption that the number, if could be calculated today, would be higher, if only because more people become aware of and comfortable with the opportunity over time.

### How did "agency pricing" change Amazon's commercial strategy?

"Agency pricing," by which publishers sold e-books directly to consumers, only using the retail as an "agent" and therefore preventing discounting, forced Amazon to change their initial e-book strategy, which made everything that was relatively attractive $9.99 or less.

The agency publishers suffered sales attrition immediately because Random House (before the Penguin merger) stayed out of agency and gave Amazon a big pool of attractive titles to price more cheaply. Then the big publishers, helped along by the courts, saw the problems with the strategy and negotiated new arrangements to "allow" some discounting by Amazon. But they often kept their set prices higher than $9.99 and had, of course, reduced the share for intermediaries from 50 percent of the retail price to 30 percent.

Amazon's response since then has been to let the big publishers be hoisted with their own petard. Amazon doesn't take the margin hit on high-priced agency e-books anymore; they are allowed to do some discounting, but they don't do it. Amazon has built up a big list of its own, has a large and growing list of indies giving them e-books on which they have price control, and, anyway, they've pretty much vanquished the e-book competition. So they no longer have the aggressive e-book discounting strategy and the agency publisher just lives with relatively lower e-book sales

### How did Amazon use terms as a catalyst to grow the self-publishing business?

When publishers invented the agency model of e-book pricing (discussed above and in Chapter 5), they put down a marker, which was that they wanted to get 70 percent of what the consumer spent on e-books. Amazon took the same number as their new royalty basis for self-published authors. Upload your e-book to them, follow certain pricing and other guidelines, and they would pay you 70 percent of the consumer price for your e-book.

Publishers by then were routinely sharing 25 percent of their e-book revenue with the author. So an Amazon indie author would make $2.10 on an e-book priced at $2.99. If a publisher priced an e-book at $9.99, the author would get 25 percent of 70 percent of that from an agency publisher, or $1.75. And, all other things being equal, a book would sell several times the number of units at such a substantially lower price.

If the print book were a $15 paperback, the author would usually get no more than 8 percent of the suggested retail price, or $1.20. So a book that cost the consumer about 80 percent less would yield almost double the revenue to the author!

For authors in the fiction genres that were really taking off in the e-book market, where print sales were steadily being diminished by e-book sales, the idea of such a high royalty on such a low price to the customer was very enticing.

Of course, Amazon could not reach *every* book reader. But when Kindle grabbed a big market share of e-book readers very quickly, it had a big enough marketplace all by itself to give a book a respectable sale within its own platform alone.

And for aspiring authors without an agent or other access to the publishers, self-publishing through Amazon was a much easier way to get a book into the marketplace. Yes, you had to deal with getting it copy-edited yourself (or else have an inferior book) and you had to create your cover. But compared to the chores of finding an agent, crafting a proposal (even if you had a complete manuscript), and living with the months of delay around submissions, negotiations, and publisher scheduling, the self-publishing requirements were not relatively onerous to many people. And those Amazon royalty rates were so much higher . . .

Once self-publishing through Amazon was made possible—and shortly after enabled by the other e-book platforms and universally to all print and digital booksellers in the world through Ingram—hundreds of thousands of titles a year were being made available through that path, bypassing the entire publishing establishment.

Indeed, one of the recent publishing phenomena—the book *Fifty Shades of Gray*—started as a self-published book and has gone on to sell millions of copies.

### How could Amazon stay competitive?

Although discounting was not a highly noticeable feature of Amazon before they slashed prices to discourage other retailers from taking advantage of Ingram's attempt to commoditize the book retailing service offering (called I2S2) in the late 1990s, forgoing margin to build customers and top line sales rapidly became the standard Amazon pricing strategy. Two things enabled that and continue to enable heavy discounting of the goods they sell to this day.

One is that Amazon very early persuaded Wall Street to look at them and value them with different standards from those they applied to all other companies. That is, Amazon said, "We are going for building up our customer base and our market share, and, by doing that, building the engine that will deliver profits in the future," and Wall Street supported a high stock price on that basis. Since Amazon used stock options as a critical component of compensation to a rapidly growing base of employees, this indulgence from Wall Street was critical. The company couldn't have continued to grow without it.

One publishing industry veteran, a senior executive of one of the major players in the ecosystem, told Mike that he thought persuading Wall Street to go along with that strategy was Jeff Bezos's most important accomplishment.

But as Amazon grew in different ways, another reality kicked in. As more of the company's revenues came from Marketplace, essentially "renting" their capability to other retailers, and then from cloud services (AWS: Amazon Web Services), the margin from actual product sales, let alone *book* sales, diminished in importance to the company.

This is a reality that many in the book business, most notably Barnes & Noble, were very slow to grasp. Without ambitions to go beyond the book business, no internet retailer in the book business could sustain a competition with Amazon. When your competitor is able to live on a much smaller margin than you need to survive, it gets very hard to compete.

### How has Amazon's publishing and strategy changed over the years?

At about the same time indie authors started flocking to Amazon to self-publish through Kindle (and then, if they wanted to, also through Amazon's CreateSpace for print book editions), Amazon started publishing.

Although the big e-book and indie author action was in genre fiction—romance, sci-fi, thrillers, mysteries, and subcategories of all of them—Amazon initially decided that their publishing imprint should go after the biggest books. To do that, they hired Larry Kirshbaum, who had headed Hachette Book Group and its predecessor Warner Books for decades and who had ubiquitous contacts among authors and agents, to get big books under contract for the newly formed Amazon Publishing.

However, getting those big books depended on Amazon's being able to secure distribution for their books outside Amazon. The enticement of advances and special marketing through the dominant online bookseller wouldn't attract really successful authors if their books wouldn't be in stores.

It turned out that Amazon had underestimated the resistance they'd face. The rest of the industry fought back. Borders was just then going out of business, but Barnes & Noble and the independent stores simply refused to stock Amazon-published books. That cut off at the knees the Kirshbaum effort to get big general books.

But genre publishing has succeeded for them very well. Amazon's own bestseller lists are overpopulated, if not dominated, by its own titles. Agents have told us that Amazon-published authors regard Amazon very highly for their attention and care. Indeed, Amazon apparently looks at all interactions with others as interactions with "customers." Authors, to them, are customers and not clients.

And, in fact, the big publishers themselves will tell you that publishing in those genres has become increasingly difficult to do successfully as a direct result of Amazon's initiatives.

As we write, the situation in the ecosystem is changing because Amazon is just starting to build a retail store presence. We believe the day will come when Amazon is both the biggest store retailer *and* the dominant online retailer. When we get there, a more general list at Amazon Publishing will probably be developed and do very well.

### How did Amazon "succeed" with a subscription offering while others failed or got little traction?

Two aggressive, non-Amazon e-book subscription offers were put into the marketplace a few years ago. One was Oyster, a venture-financed start-up that has since disappeared. Oyster tried to compete on price, couldn't build up a subscriber base fast enough, and ran out of cash.

The other one was from Scribd, a document archiving, commenting, and publishing service that built an e-book subscription platform as an adjunct. They lasted longer but ultimately found they couldn't support the "one price for all you want from our repository" model, so they modified it to make it less generous.

Meanwhile, Amazon has built Kindle Unlimited. From the beginning, Amazon decided how much money to allocate each month for "reads" in that service and divided it up among the participating books by pages read. They have very little in the way of top-flight commercial books in the service, but they also have lots of customers and lots of titles and a sustainable model that keeps many consumers happy outside the reach of the retailers and for most e-books not within their system.

### How did Amazon start to affect the new title business and bestseller lists?

The big publishers have become increasingly scientific in positioning their real candidates for the bestseller lists to have the best chance of getting on them. And the single biggest key to that is the first week sale, as discussed in Chapter 3.

The most reliable way to build a first week sale is with preorders on Amazon, which will certainly ship the day the book first goes on sale. And the publishers' efforts to make sure all big books have big first weeks at Amazon becomes another aspect of their competitive advantage. Amazon already had a special place in sales of backlist because they never had the "in stock" challenge that the physical bookstore has. But the new reality is that Amazon is also the most important account on the day the book comes out, which assures that they get the publishers' full attention—and help from their promotion budgets—from their earliest marketing moments.

Now that we've taken a tour of the marketplace, let us drill down into some specific areas of publishing that are distinct, starting with children's publishing and young adult publishing.

# 8

# CHILDREN'S AND YOUNG ADULT (YA) PUBLISHING

*Why is children's book publishing so often viewed as a world apart from adult publishing?*

You can tell if someone doesn't work in children's publishing if she can't tell you the difference between the Caldecott and Newbery Awards. The American Library Association (ALA) awards the Caldecott for books with illustrations, and it awards the Newbery for literature. Children's publishing insiders know this delineation by heart, whereas others will give you a blank look if asked to distinguish between the two.

Maybe surprising to publishing outsiders, there is very little crossover between publishing staffs for kids' and adult books. People tend to have careers in one or the other and don't go back and forth. In many essential ways, they really are different businesses. The most obvious reason is that for one category, the primary user is a child, and for a quarter or more of the children's books sold the end user is not the reader but a listener, as a parent, caregiver, or teacher does the actual reading. An essay in the January 1888 issue of the *Atlantic* reminds us that reading to children goes back as far as time itself.

In discussing publishing for kids of the day, no less a figure than Samuel Johnson gives his opinion on what to read to children. "Babies do not want," said he, "to hear about babies; they like to be told of giants and castles and of somewhat which can stretch and stimulate their little minds." And then remember always, that the parents buy the books, and that the children never read them.

The transition to books children can read on their own is generally the transition from picture books (lavishly illustrated large-format books with little text) to what publishers call chapter books (traditional trim-sized books divided into chapters and dominated by words, with occasional illustrations). This shift makes children feel a real sense of independence and maturity. Many of us remember when we started reading chapter books and the excitement that brought.

One of the most important pieces of information on a kids' book cover is the target age group for the title; there is an art to matching the book's content to this age range, and it varies by book format.

### Do backlist and classic titles have a greater impact on children's books than in adult trade?

Yes, because, for one thing, the target audience rotates constantly. Today's children grow out of a group of titles only to be replaced by a new target audience in subsequent years. So what is old is truly new again. While new titles are constantly added to the backlist, the miracle of the most popular children's books remaining popular year after year is in part because there is less turnover in the reading decision makers. Parents have subsequent children and favorite titles are reused or repurchased, parents become grandparents repeating the dynamic, and last, children become parents with an almost biological imperative to relive their childhoods by reading favorite titles to their children.

*What about kids' publishing accounts for such consistent sales growth in recent years?*

Sales growth in children's publishing outpaced growth in adult publishing in virtually all adult print formats from 2012 to 2016. The most recent Nielsen Bookscan numbers as of this writing say that children's books grew twice as quickly as adult books from 2005 to 2015, a 4 percent compound annual growth rate versus 2 percent for adult books. This period of growth is significant as it occurred in traditional retail as well as in more discrete school and library markets for kids' titles. Online sales grew at a more modest rate.

In spite of this industry growth, which might suggest radical changes in marketing and sales, new titles in children's publishing are still introduced to the marketplace in a time-honored way.

Kids' reading habits in the K–8 years are driven by librarians, teachers, and often parents. And children's book publishers leverage this, by providing ARCs (advance reading copies) to teachers and librarians as well as making available to them posters and other collateral material to help spur interest in certain books. By influencing the influencers, the most trusted source of word-of-mouth communication there is on which books a child should read, publishers are able to build a strong gateway to parents and kids.

Interestingly, while email direct to kids would almost certainly be the most effective technique, the law prohibits collecting names of those thirteen or under.

*What is the difference between children's and young adult (YA) books and how do these markets compare?*

What we call "children's" here is sometimes thought of as two pieces: "Early Childhood/I Can Read" and "Middle

Grade." Young adult is for teens, young people who read very much on their own and also often choose their own books. The biggest growth in the last three years has been board books (for young kids) and nonfiction. YA has flattened, but those numbers are trickier because YA is sometimes, even often, read by adults, and many actual young adults read regular adult books. The short distinction is that children's publishing is for kids too young to make their own purchasing decisions, and young adult publishing is aimed at young people making these decisions for themselves. Selling children's books requires marketing to the influencers—parents and teachers. Young adult books, particularly in the internet age, are found by kids themselves in their vast online world.

There are rules about marketing to minors, and minors often don't have credit cards. But the publisher aims its marketing efforts at the decision makers, and for young adult books, for the first time, that's the kids themselves.

*Has the increasing crossover of adults reading more sophisticated kids' titles and kids reading titles published for adults further contributed to the success of kids' titles?*

Anecdotally, teenagers have often gone beyond the YA titles published specifically for them and have been reading Danielle Steel, Stephen King, Nora Roberts, and others. But what has contributed to the growth in the children's market has been the success of major series titles like the *Harry Potter, Twilight,* and *The Hunger Games* books. A Nielson Books and Consumer Survey indicates that 65 percent of the buyers of young adult titles were males eighteen to forty-four. And 65 percent of those adults reported buying the books for themselves, not children, as reported by Alexandra Alter in the *New York Times*, April 10, 2015.

*How are children's and YA books sold?*

In addition to the traditional vendors like online and brick-and-mortar book stores, school book fairs and school book clubs provide unique and highly popular ways of reaching young readers. Sales through those channels at Scholastic Inc. alone reached $745 million dollars in the fiscal year ending June 2017, accounting for 70 percent of the sales of Scholastic's children's trade division. Books are sold directly to parents (through vehicles that enable the actual "shopping" and "selection" to be done by students). Titles for book clubs are chosen from a catalog and are delivered by mail order or a combination of mail order and packages delivered direct to classrooms. For the book fairs, the sales happen on-site, with parents invited to visit the school, much in the way of a bake sale.

The books sold through these two nontraditional models are a mix of titles licensed from all publishers and Scholastic's own originated titles. They can have dramatically discounted prices as they are generally different from the retail editions by being printed on less expensive paper and having less costly bindings. They are, however, the introduction to some children's authors and characters for many kids and go on to stimulate future sales through traditional channels.

Also setting the children's and YA market apart is Amazon's comparatively smaller share of the market, compared to their dominance in other segments of publishing. Children's publishers we spoke with said that Amazon has been slower in figuring out how to sell kids' titles that are often heavily illustrated, tactile in how they are constructed, and sometimes uniquely three-dimensional. The mechanics of how to display them on screen and communicate these differences, and then how to lure customers to them is not yet optimal for Amazon.

This makes sense, as people currently interact with children's bookstore spaces in a variety of ways: reading to children there and spending more time shopping with kids, seeing how certain formats and colors and texts appeal to their child. Ultimately this helps kids to acclimatize themselves to print books and to reading from an early age. As yet, it is hard to replicate these experiences online in a way that is as meaningful for parents or children.

### Where has social media been effective in the publicity and marketing of children's books?

The world of YA fiction, either published in paperback, in e-book format, or in a digital e-book, has found that social media networks can be a productive venue for speaking directly to their reading audience. The YA authors' websites and blogs appear to develop organically, with their readers welcoming a place to share views, gossip, and opinions. Even the casting of a character or narrator on an author's new audiobook, when it contains a personality that crosses over into the author's audience, creates excitement and buzz that redounds back to the print and e-book versions of the title.

### Is the acquisition and editorial development process different for kids' books than for adult books?

The process is not only generally different from that of adult trade publishing but in fact tends to differ for each format of children's publishing: picture books, chapter books, and YA—which is most likely published in trade paperback but at times in mass-market paperback. The kids' book world may include many of the same publishing houses (and certainly all of the Big Five), but the processes and players are really different. If you were an author submitting a kids' title for publication, you would want to use a literary agent familiar with the kids' book world and with the different cast of characters in the juvenile book business.

For illustrated books, you may not be required to submit sample artwork, or you may be submitting it only to get across the idea of the style you envision. The editor and others at the house may well prefer to handle the art, using someone they have experience with and who they feel will be able to work well with their creative direction. This developmental process can be a long and arduous one as the editor, the illustrator, and the author strive to bring out the value in the text. The developmental process can frequently run longer than the year that is the average for adult book production, In fact, the creative process for an illustrated kids' trade title frequently takes over eighteen months to complete.

### How do young readers prefer to read?

Many people, especially older readers, assume that kids and teens prefer digital formats for everything, including reading, but this might not be the case. The children's publishers we interviewed were surprised by their finding that kids have not switched their book reading from printed books to their phones or e-readers. They are reading printed books at or around the same rate they always did and are using their digital devices for phone/text messages/video media, not as substitutes for print books.

# 9

# AUDIOBOOKS

***What is the current landscape of audiobook publishing?***

Audiobooks, whose first organized venture in the form of recordings for the blind came at the same time as mass-market paperbacks, are now coming into their own as the fastest growing segment of trade publishing, after a period of lesser popularity.

With a shift to downloading audiobooks rather than using CDs or tapes, the average age of audiobook users has changed. The Audio Publishers Association survey says that frequent audio listeners are under the age of thirty-five. And overall the users are about 90 percent adults, which makes sense given the visual nature of so many books for children. These data differ dramatically from the rule-of-thumb age for the average book reader and bookstore buyer, who is always said to be fifty-five and up. If even directionally true it might mean that there is a significant upside to digital audio.

Even so, many readers have a strange prejudice against audiobooks. Although listening to books read aloud is as old as books themselves, and almost all of us were read to as children—at home or in school—it seems hard to believe that probably the biggest remaining obstacle in the audio publishing industry is overcoming reader reluctance to accept the format. (We discuss the prejudices against audiobooks later in this chapter.)

Like mass-market paperbacks and e-books, audio titles are over 75 percent fiction, with the most popular genres being mysteries/thrillers/suspense, science fiction/fantasy, and romance.

### Who are the key players in the audiobook industry?

Aside from Library of Congress efforts at building a collection of audiobooks for the blind that began in the 1930s, the companies that were in on the early development of audio were Caedmon Records, Listening Library, and Spoken Arts. They were the three early entrants in the 1950s and '60s. Books on Tape was founded in 1971 as a direct-to-consumer mail-order rental business and was bought by Random House in 2001. Two years later, Recorded Books was founded; it remains a stand-alone subsidiary of an investment group to this day but was just sold by one to another in July 2018. Brilliance Audio was another independent audio player that was purchased by Amazon and integrated into their audio suite.

Slowly but surely the large publishers through growth or acquisition built up their audio operations. Some are organized at the imprint level; others, like Simon & Schuster, Penguin Random House, and Hachette Book Group, have corporate audio operations that are fed content by all of the divisions.

### Why are many readers resistant to audiobooks?

If asked, many people will simply say, "I don't use audiobooks." Not "I don't read them" or "I don't listen to them," but "I don't *use* them." This seems to show that they are thought of as a different sort of object than a book, a different activity from reading. In the minds of many, hearing an audiobook is closer to listening to a podcast—something you're either into or not, but that's also seeing a boom—than it is to picking up a print or e-book.

Most of the people we know who are not addicted from birth to listening to audio editions prove very hard to convert. Author Robert Riger managed the Pimsleur language programs at Simon & Schuster's audio division for seven years when the company was very generous in providing employees with sample copies of new audio titles as they came in from the duplicator (which was the hard-copy audio version of "the printer"). Since he didn't personally *use* audiobooks, he brought them to friends as gifts, and with very few exceptions they made all the right thank-you noises and then asked if they could trade the audio for the hardcover.

There has historically quite often been a sense that new iterations of words on or around a page are not "real" books (and that reading them is somehow cheating). This charge is leveled against some books based on their tone or genre, and others based on their format. Everything from William Faulkner's style, to the book clubs that were founded in the 1920s, to the Pocket Book revolution, to shopping in chain bookstores and then online bookstores, e-books and now audiobooks have been said to be less than real books and looked down on.

Audiobooks are perhaps the most different of all the new formats and venues, and they have also suffered from the perception that all audiobooks except multivolume library editions have been casually abridged, slashed at random to fit some length and price formula. The truth is that in 2016, according to the Audio Publishers Association, abridged audiobooks represented only 3.8 percent of all units sold, down from almost 10 percent in 2012. In fact, digital audio liberated the format from the physical limitations that mandated the abridgments in the first place. Because they have led the trade industry in percentage sales growth three years running, audiobooks are once again attracting the attention, sometimes negative, of the purists.

When the *New York Times* wrote its first audiobook culture piece in 1985, the lead described a stockbroker who used his new portable cassette player to listen to Thoreau's *Walden* while weeding his Connecticut garden. The hook for the piece and the anticipated hook for the success of audio titles in general was the human ability to multitask: in this case, gardening while listening to a book read aloud.

Jonathan Kozol, then the primary critic of America's inadequate educational system, was the resident curmudgeon in this piece, focused largely on the notion that all audiobooks are abridged (and many more were then than are now), but he also managed a poetic put-down: "Tapes are one more disincentive to literacy," said Mr. Kozol. "In the case of serious works of art, there is something precious about the silence that surrounds reading. In the case of books of opinion, it is far more difficult to maintain a fine, critical edge when exposed to the quick-fix, toil-free process of listening."

In a more robust *New York Times* piece on the cultural validity of the audiobook published twenty years after the first, Mr. Kozol has been replaced by the archangel of the bound book: "Deep reading really demands the inner ear as well as the outer ear," said Harold Bloom, the literary critic. "You need the whole cognitive process, that part of you which is open to wisdom. You need the text in front of you."

This led us to wonder if there was anything to this idea that the brain does not engage content from a book as fully when it comes in through the ears rather than through the eyes.

## Is listening to an audiobook "cheating?"

Many still feel that it is—that you haven't truly read something if you've merely listened to it. Daniel Willingham, professor of psychology at the University of Virginia, has researched the brain basis of learning and memory, and in recent years he has applied that research to K–16 education. Willingham has some interesting insights on this issue:

" Listening to an audio book may have more information [provided by the articulation and intonation of a reader] that will make comprehension a little easier. Prosody might clarify the meaning of ambiguous words or help you to assign syntactic roles to words. But most of the time it doesn't, because most of what you listen to is not that complicated. For most books, for most purposes, listening and reading are more or less the same thing. So listening to an audiobook is not 'cheating,' but let me tell you why I objected to phrasing the question that way. 'Cheating' implies an unfair advantage, as though you are receiving a benefit while skirting some work. Why talk about reading as though it were work?"

## What technological advances have enabled the spread of audiobooks?

The audio industry has been propelled forward by various milestones in listening technology, from the cassette player through the iPhone. Once cars had an installed base of cassette players in the 1970s and then CD players in the 1990s, the lion's share of audiobook listening happened in drive time, the perfect mix of a need for something to occupy part of the driver's mind, lack of interruptions, and a quiet space the listener can control. Point-of-sales data in 2008 showed that audiobook sales took their biggest one-time hit during the year of record high gasoline prices. Driving was reduced, so listening and sales were reduced.

With the proliferation of portable digital audio devices that enable direct-to-device downloads and then a built-in way to listen to audiobooks, the drive time usage is down to 32 percent and "at home" listening has risen to 57 percent of sales.

### How does Audible, the industry leader, stand out from the rest of the audio industry?

First and foremost, Audible, now Amazon's audiobook arm, is a technology company at heart, having started out in 1998, two years after opening its doors, by launching a digital audio player some four years before the iPod came out. It was limited in what it could hold but had the seeds of the company's philosophy in effect to this day of uniquely encrypted DRM—digital rights management software that prevents unauthorized copying—on virtually everything digital that the company sells. A few years later Audible made a deal with Apple to have their books on the iTunes store. They began publishing exclusive titles in 2008. Also in 2008, Amazon bought Audible for $300 million.

To ensure that the Audible sales engine would have sufficient titles, under Amazon they formed a production company called Audio Book Creation Exchange that operates as a production vehicle connecting independents with the talent needed to make audiobooks.

Audible's marketing also sets them apart. Almost exclusively, when you join Audible, you join a subscription marketing plan, and each month you are billed a subscription fee for which you receive one or two audio credits. Each book in Audible's catalog has a value in credits, translated from the retail price; customers don't need to buy something each month but can strategically save their credits to have enough for a particular book.

From our perspective, the smartest thing Audible has done is to implement a spin on the old book club "get a member" programs, which always were the least expensive and best-performing source of new members for book clubs. Audible's program was called Onebook, which enabled its subscribers to send a book in their library to up to ten different people. If recipients were not subscribers and this was their first-ever Audible title, the donor got a free audiobook. Apparently, it was so successful that last year it was radically expanded and renamed Send-a-Book, and the original Audible subscriber can now share a book with up to 1,000 people. Those people still get one free book, which they can now share with other people in their network, and if they have an Amazon account they are not forced into a thirty-day trial.

In addition, a current Audible TV commercial ends with an offer that you respond to by a series of simple key strokes on your cell phone, signing you up to a trial version of their subscription program. Historically, the need for articulating fine print would have prevented this, but with the cell phone interface, the company is able to cover the contractual issues and the cautionary terms on the phone screen before you complete your enrollment. For a business that once lived and breathed on its truck stop sales, when its largest audience was composed of people stuck in vehicles for long periods of time, this is clearly a new age.

### How is the product development process different for audiobooks and readable books?

Creating audiobooks is a much bigger challenge than simply transforming hardcover books into a new format after all the editorial and design choices have been made in the production of the original print version and, in fact, a digital file exists that can pretty easily "spit out" a different format for putting the words on new paper or screen "page" sizes. In fact, the audio division is at the mercy of the originating imprint and the author, since most of the work in producing the audio cannot begin until the underlying manuscript is locked, and then as the packaging is usually designed to amplify the look of the hardcover, it too has to be final before the audio creative process can move forward.

In fact, producers of audiobooks need a whole cadre of people to edit and prep a book for recording. Many new creative decisions are required to create audiobooks, not least of which is deciding who will do the reading.

It can take seventeen hours of audio, delivered via download or in a chunky box of CDs, to completely read what was originally a 450-page book. And the industry rule of thumb is 6.2 hours of studio time for every finished hour of audio. That includes the narrator's recording time, editing time, and then quality control. What is significant is that the cost of production for an average unabridged title has come down from an average of $25,000 in the '70s and '80s to between $2,500 and $5,000 now.

Some of the larger houses have been trying out narrators who have home studios and could conceivably make recording books into a cottage industry. This would cost the publishers even less while allowing them to produce more titles without increasing studio overhead. Add to that the savings from selling 82 percent of the product as a digital download versus many CDs in a box and the $75 price for an unabridged audio in cassette format is a thing of the past.

The evolving content creation and consumption world fostered by handheld devices and ubiquitous Wi-Fi connections creates inherent barriers to long-form reading and inherent wind at the back of audiobooks. They're cheaper to make than they ever were before and they're now very easy—just as easy as spelled-out words—to deliver as well. It seems reasonable to expect that long-form books will gradually decline and long-form audio will grab a larger share of consumer attention for many years to come.

# 10

# THE FUTURE OF PUBLISHING

*What is the impact of nontraditional sales on the trade book industry?*

This book has focused on how traditional trade publishing operates today within the confines of the historical functions of publishing companies. We've addressed the growth of e-book publishing by trade publishers and the sea change that Amazon's dominant role in trade publishers' book sales has wrought.

What we've not yet addressed is the $1.25 billion consumer nontraditional US book industry—books created by individuals or entities that are not commercial publishers—that accounted for 297 million units sold in 2016. This is a full 20 percent of the roughly $6 billion traditional US trade book market.

According to Data Guy, who has developed a unique way of tracking traditional and nontraditional trade book sales, the nontraditional titles were nonexistent until 2011. Then, "between 2011 and 2013, the non-traditional share expanded rapidly from near-zero to a full 25–30 percent of all eBook units sold in the US (although a substantially smaller percentage of gross consumer eBook dollars), even as the overall size of the eBook market itself was growing rapidly)," according to Data Guy's Author

Earnings blog. From 2014 to 2016, he notes the agency agreements that the Big Five houses signed resulted in their reporting shrinking e-book sales, while Amazon was simultaneously reporting e-books growing in both units and dollars. The insistence on maintaining a semblance of historical pricing from traditional publisher sales further fueled the rise of the nontraditional industry. The fact that over half (54 percent) of all trade e-book sales units could be published by "nontraditional" sources within five years of the nontraditional sources' first real appearance in sales tracking, and that 22 percent of all trade units could be represented by nontraditional sales in the same time frame, is staggering.

### What is Amazon's role in nontraditional publishing?

Amazon is directly responsible for 22 percent of all the nontraditional units in a somewhat traditional way— books published by their rather traditionally curated imprints: Montlake, Thomas Mercer, 47 North, Skyscape, Amazon Crossing, and Two Lions; for audiobooks the major producers are Audio Studio and Brilliance Audio (as described in Chapter 9).

The bulk of the units from the Amazon self-publishing options can be found on Amazon.com's footer information, under the heading "Make Money with Us"—and then accessed by clicking the link "Self-Publish with Us"; this click takes you to the page that offers different tools for e-book, print, and audio self-publishing.

Their overall pitch is to "Take Control with Self-Publishing," using Kindle Direct Publishing to "publish your book for free and reach millions of readers, earn royalties of up to 70 percent, easily publish in just minutes and have the book on Amazon sites within just two days, and sell it worldwide."

Their print option is offered through Amazon CreateSpace, which has "easy-to-use independent publishing tools, everything to create, publish and distribute your book for free." Again, the watchword is that the author retains control, as well as stressing speed to market and global distribution. How you make a print book for free isn't immediately apparent.

For audio, you use ACX, which is Audible's marketplace "where authors, literary agents, publishers, and other Rights Holders can connect with narrators, engineers, recording studios, and other Producers capable of producing a finished audiobook." The audio process is inherently more difficult and complex than self-publishing a print or e-book and is the one nontraditional format that produces fewer units on the self-publishing side, 28 percent of the audio nontraditional sales versus all self-published units that add up to 77 percent of nontraditional sales.

### What does self-publishing look like beyond Amazon?

The lion's share—more than half in almost all cases and more than 80 percent in many, as far as we can tell—of indie book sales are through Amazon; however, they are not alone trying to serve the indie author and fledgling publisher.

### What does the nontraditional publishing world look like beyond Amazon?

Although Amazon dominates this market, some choose to publish through channels beyond Amazon because Amazon doesn't reach other bookstores much at all, doesn't reach other e-book formats, and really hardly scratches the surface on libraries with print books.

Self-publishers would maximize their e-book revenues by individually loading the e-book on each self-publishing platform: B&N Nook, Kobo, Apple iBooks, Google Play, and even a smaller marketer like Smashwords. If you go directly to each of these platforms, you will pay no fee to a distributor.

However, since the combined e-book sales of all these others will probably be less than Amazon in total, many publishers would choose to reach the other platforms through an aggregator. Ingram is the one most frequently used, but Smashwords will take you to other platforms as will service companies like Draft2Digital.

Self-publishers use print-on-demand for physical books because they rarely have a way to shift a press-run quantity efficiently. There are three print-on-demand operations. Amazon owns CreateSpace. You would use CreateSpace because Amazon sells your print books and that's the most efficient way to reach their audience. But other retailers tend to resist buying from Amazon.

Donnelley, the biggest printer in the world, also provides print-on-demand capability. But they have no "customers" or delivery capability. Using Donnelly makes sense if you have a market you can reach for the books and only need a printer, but it is not a solution to reach the wider marketplace.

By far the biggest provider of printed books—mostly through one-at-a-time print-on-demand—for indies is Ingram's venerable Lightning Print operation. It is now twenty years old, and Ingram makes it easy for anybody to access through their online Ingram Spark portal. Books set up with Lightning appear with Ingram as "in stock" when a bookstore or library searches their database. And this is achieved without the publisher having to print or hold any inventory.

### What drives self-publishing?

It's one thing to imagine people going for this new model of self-publishing (free or low cost, immediate, built-in access to a large market of readers, royalty upside) versus the vanity publishing model of yore (pseudo-hardcover, obscenely expensive, slow turnaround, and then author's burden of marketing and sales, not to mention the requirement of a large garage to store books you'll never sell). It's quite another to imagine these titles collectively selling almost 300 million units that generated $1.25 billion in sales in 2016. This means that consumers spent real money—to buy and read untold pages of books written and uploaded directly into the cultural bloodstream with no judgment, mediation, review, or pitching by the traditional keepers of the gate.

What's different about these books? They get to see the light of day without anyone saying, "It's really just a magazine article," or "I can't see how we'd position it—as it's part poor man's Grisham, YA Grafton, with a dash of Sherlock Holmes abridged by Reader's Digest," or "The numbers just don't work; we've tried to sell African American fiction time and time again and can't forecast sales that will cover the overhead," or any of the hundred or so ways books are routinely judged and dismissed in traditional publishing. Maintaining the idea that having a traditional publisher agree to publish your book with even the smallest advance is as remote as winning a lottery certainly helps to feed the self-published pipeline.

The digital self-publishing route allows authors who realize that the deck is stacked against them if they enter the traditional literary lottery to get immediate feedback from this new pool of consumers with a demonstrated willingness to sample and then read "unbranded" material. The filter from the publishing elite, and from booksellers is gone. Despite absurdly low unit prices (which is, of course, their first selling point and entrée to their customers' consideration), the two components of nontraditional publishing have built a $1.25 billion (consumer) business in five short years.

### How do traditional and nontraditional e-book sales trends compare?

When you drill down into the subject areas of publishing that are driving the growth in the new formats, distribution outlets, and new sources of titles, there is an immediate sense of déjà-vu in the core book categories that dominate these new areas of publishing.

In a conversation about why e-books as a percentage of traditional publisher sales had stalled just as they had reached the mid-20 percent range, publishing industry sage Michael Cader pointed out that e-book sales were anything but evenly distributed across the titles on a publisher's list. He insisted that we examine e-book sales by category to get a true picture of this new publishing format.

The e-books that had led the growth in the new format for traditional publishers were general and category fiction titles, and those same titles continued their growth even when the overall e-book share of publisher sales had retrenched. This is spelled out by the fact that 49 percent of traditional publishers' adult fiction unit sales in 2016 were represented by e-books and audio sales. To further cement this trend, when you look at all traditional and nontraditional adult fiction 2016 sales units together, a full 70 percent of those sales are composed of e-book and audio sales. And when all nontraditional sales are aggregated, 42 percent of them are adult fiction titles, according to Data Guy.

As you dig deeper into the individual genres/categories of adult fiction that are self-published independently, you find wide differences in their share of what are largely e-book titles versus their share of what the traditional publishers manage to publish and sell.

We can observe some interesting trends by looking at which areas thrive within self-published fiction. Romance, a huge category overall selling 156 million units compared to African American's 12 million, is now 96 percent e-books, and a controlling share of these—55 percent of romance units—are self-published independently. At a future date it would be fascinating to study the shift from the mass-market paperback-dominated romance industry to the robust e-book-controlled romance world of today.

Science-fiction, horror, and action adventure are the three categories ranked next, each with close to 40 percent of the independent self-published market. With these three lead fiction categories and mystery and thrillers bringing up the rear totaling 45 percent, the sense of déjà vu grows stronger and stronger.

### How does this nontraditional phenomenon fit into the history of publishing?

Here's the deal: for virtually every new distribution channel or new publishing format since the seventeenth century when the ubiquity of movable type allowed publishers to pre-sell long expensive works in low-cost installments known as "Fascicles," the early adopting consumers have been the book addicts, the readers who have not been able to get enough of a narrative fix at the frequency they need it and at a price they can afford from the traditional outlets. Beginning with Charles Dickens's *Pickwick Papers* in 1836, which was serialized in twenty stand-alone parts at a shilling apiece, as time went by serializations were printed in newspapers and magazines where readers could sometimes get parts of two novels in one magazine for the price of the partwork.

George Eliot, Willkie Collins, Thomas Hardy, and Anthony Trollope were serialized in the United Kingdom, and Harriet Beecher Stowe, Mark Twain, Henry James, and many others had serialized works in the United States. Serials actually altered the writer's editorial output. Most didn't write the whole book and then have it sliced in even pieces to be serialized in the future. Due partly to the immediate audience feedback, and to human nature, these serials were written more like weekly or monthly newspaper columns with suspenseful cliffhangers at the end of many of the installments. It took a particular kind of author, and the output of those writers was at the core of what we know as the nineteenth-century novel. Most important from our perspective, it was a wholly new format that efficiently fed an old hunger among the most voracious readers.

Again and again book dealers (publishers, booksellers, or new entrants like book clubs and online retailers) have devised new ways of feeding the hunger of these users, who because of the high volume of their consumption are often seen as indiscriminate book consumers and looked down on by the traditional publishers of the day.

### How were book clubs received as a nontraditional business?

This disdain for the new, or for outsiders, is often leveled at the inventors of the new methods of book distribution—who often are inclined to start with the most popular genres—as well. At the outset, the book clubs were set upon for claiming to be able to choose the best book each month: "The greater the number of subscribers, the greater the greater the need of close attention on the part of the club managements to the acceptability of their selections to the average taste of their subscribers with a probable downward tendency in quality," said Frederick Stokes, president of the Frederick Stokes Company in the *New York Times*, who with E. P. Dutton refused to submit their books to the newly formed Book-of-the-Month Club and the Literary Guild in 1929.

The fascinating thing about the infighting over the book clubs was that the usual "stealing our lunch" arguments that face any new nontraditional book channel were almost always combined with rants against "catering to the lowest common denominator in Americans' reading taste"; it was as though fighting on the commercial plane was beneath the publishers, but if they could defeat this nascent form of book distribution by impugning its literary value all the better. Book-of-the-Month Club either anticipated this fight or started it by installing a board of judges with impeccable literary pedigrees who were to pick each month's selection.

More important on the sales front, the millions of dollars the book clubs quickly generated came largely from fiction and, as time went by, from romance, mystery, science fiction, and historical fiction; the Literary Guild even developed subsidiary clubs that were exclusively devoted to each genre. These categories map very closely to those now driving the nontraditional business.

### What does the history of mass-market paperbacks have in common with today's new formats?

After book clubs had become established, the next great nontraditional publishing wave was of course the mass-market paperback revolution—the "dime-novels," "pocket-books," or—in industry parlance—"rack-sized" paperbacks that began to impact the industry in earnest in 1939, only a decade or so after the book clubs first shook things up.

Both clubs and paperbacks are credited with expanding the universe of readers in the United States beyond the traditional booksellers and libraries. The clubs used mail order (negative option distribution—you get the book we're telling you about unless you actively tell us not to send it—in exchange for free books up front; members agreed to discounted automatic delivery of the club's choice) and the brilliant expansion to news agents by accepting their distribution mechanisms whereby books were placed on racks automatically (with returns required of covers only for credit) rather than chosen by booksellers one by one.

The categories with the most success as paperback reprints were the subgenres of general fiction (including classics), and as paperback originals took over the racks the categories were dominated by romance, mystery, science-fiction, and thrillers—again the core categories that dominate all the other new channels and formats in publishing. And again this new book format was increasingly accessible at a dramatically lower price to readers who were never without a book, and also to wider reading audience who did not have access to bookstores or as likely were shy of running the gauntlet that faces customers unused to a traditional bookstore.

### How are audiobooks related to the other new formats?

Next in the history of publishing disruptors were audiobooks, the sales of which are also skewed to these fiction categories. Here there is no price break, but there is an increase in accessibility for the reader who may have issues reading straight text. Audio is truly a new work, infused with drama and interpretation and color that makes it appeal to different consumers than those who prefer straight text. In fact, the reverse is also true. It's just a different experience. Many, if not most, straight text readers do not cross over to audio, as we saw Chapter 9.

### What will be the ultimate impact of nontraditional publishing?

All the above-mentioned nontraditional formats have seemed as if they would swamp the traditional business at different times, but instead each has peaked in popularity and the voracious readers have then either shifted to a new format or have been supplanted demographically by a new crop of readers looking for a way to slake their insatiable demand with a format or delivery mechanism that works for them, at a price they can afford. We may likely see the same hold true for current nontraditional publishing, which is mainly self-published e-books.

Once an author gets in the door of the industry, perhaps via the shiny new indie channel, there is no reason that writer wouldn't be sought after and enticed by the full line of sales and author services—editing, promotion, and cover design, not to mention money up front—offered by a traditional publishing house. This is one reason that Amazon and other nontraditional service vendors emphasize the idea that "You are in control." And the Amazon royalty deal is best for authors if they keep their titles exclusive with Amazon.

Making a standard trade deal means the author will get broader distribution, but the price of the book will go up to the consumer (costing sales) and the share of the price that goes to the author will diminish sharply. Nonetheless, some authors find self-publishing a path to finding a publisher and, for many, the trade-off of greater exposure and having a publisher to do all the "work" is well worth the reduction in revenue per unit sold.

It is interesting that of all of these nontraditional additions to the trade publishing business, only the current wave of self-published books is by definition composed of entirely original content from the outset (paperback originals came in the second wave); how that content adapts to sales and reader interests over time will likely determine how much more market share it can capture. And it is true that some self-published output is of books previously put out by houses whose rights have been reclaimed by the authors.

### Of today's companies, which are likely to be important components of the trade book business in ten years?

Three companies that are significant players in today's book business are well positioned to benefit from the additional changes and consolidation we'll see in the coming years. They are Amazon, Penguin Random House, and Ingram.

### What makes Amazon's position so strong?

Amazon controls the sales to more end users, by *far*, than any other entity in the world. Not only are they now selling about half or more of the books published by traditional houses in the United States and 70 percent or more of the nontraditional titles being published but, with significant penetration worldwide, they know more *about* their customers than any other entity.

This has given them a virtually unassailable position for online book sales, print or digital. Now they are leveraging their proprietary supply chain—far larger and far-reaching and more sophisticated than that of any other retailer— to experiment with physical stores of various sizes and formats. Having achieved online dominance, they are now expanding their physical shelf space for books when virtually every other established book retailer is reducing it.

With their acquisition of retailer Whole Foods and the elements needed for a drug store business combined with their existing knowledge of what book buyers buy across their product line, we look for Amazon to make cross-selling books with other product lines a cornerstone of their retail operations.

At the same time, Amazon has become the go-to resource for independent authors and publishers, offering a one-stop opportunity to reach a majority of book buyers. Not only do they sell individual print and digital books, but they also offer the only e-book subscription service that is broad-based and growing. And they reward those authors or publishers who will make their content available exclusively on the Amazon platform, further consolidating their position as the retailer-of-choice for the consumer, who will find content on Amazon that isn't available anywhere else.

### What makes Penguin Random House's position so strong?

Today there are five major US consumer publishers capable of publishing books in all formats and in all topics and consistently delivering bestsellers. They are Penguin Random House, HarperCollins, Hachette, Macmillan, and Simon & Schuster. The last three are all about the same size, in the middle triple digit millions in annual sales. Harper Collins is about the size of all three of them, or about $2 billion in sales. And Penguin Random House is about the size of all four of them put together, or about $4 billion in sales.

That has meant that PRH can take more risks and put more muscle behind more books than the other Big Five publishers combined. They have used their strength to build proprietary audience reach—through email lists and topical or vertical Web presences—that the others can't match. What they have not done yet, although the threat is always there that they might, is establish PRH-only retail outlets that shut out the other publishers. (One former CEO of one of the other four told Mike that, of course, he would make his bestsellers available to PRH for their proprietary distribution should they establish something like that.) How that would fly with consumers, and what would the retail business model be—number of stock-keeping units, retail square footage, stand-alone, mall store, or main street—are the variables PRH would have to tackle to try something like this.

PRH would be right to be sensitive about being too aggressive and being perceived as "too big" for fair competition. But they also have a strong ethic of support for the trade book infrastructure and they would undermine their bookstore customers if they created many outlets for their content that shut out other publishers but also competed with bookstores. (Amazon has no such concerns.)

Like all its competitors, PRH distributes the books of other publishers as well as their own. This is a necessary component of publishers' businesses in the modern era because print book sales, particularly outside Amazon, are inexorably declining and all publishers need more "throughput" to make their operations—warehouses and fulfillment systems and field sales organizations—commercially viable. Investing in more titles in the face of declining sales is not attractive; renting one's services to utilize their overheads is seen as a more sensible approach.

PRH touches more accounts with greater frequency than any other publisher. They can offer the best distribution services so they tend to get the best distribution clients. At the same time, they have the biggest kitty for pursuing the big books for publication. The combination of those two things suggests that they will continue to grow and, in the immediate future, are likely to do so at the direct expense of the other Big Five houses. It might be difficult for the government to accept PRH buying one of those competitors, but it is just as difficult for the government to stop PRH from inexorably expanding its author base at the expense of those competitors. And the government would have to keep in mind that when it sued Random House's (then) competitors over agency pricing, they strengthened what is now PRH and Amazon, and weakened everybody else.

### What makes Ingram's position so strong?

Ingram began in life as a "wholesaler": a company that "carries" in its warehouse the books of many publishers to allow stores and libraries to purchase the books of many publishers through one vendor. Over the past four decades, the company has expanded its service offerings considerably as a distributor and a provider of short-run printing services, as well as a host of digital services, many aimed at the college market.

Since Ingram's explosive growth that resulted from delivering its inventory to stores on microfiche in the 1970s, it has sold books to more commercial accounts than anybody in the world. Since it developed Lightning Source and really started the print-on-demand capability for the industry in the late 1990s, Ingram has been the source for what are now *double-digit millions* of titles that get manufactured only when Ingram gets an order for them. Although Amazon also does print-on-demand through their CreateSpace-branded network of printers, and global printing giant R. R. Donnelley has also developed this capability, Ingram has far more titles and is the dominant supplier of these titles to most accounts in the world. Many retailers are uncomfortable stocking books that are supplied by Amazon, and Donnelley really has no wholesaling network.

Ingram's other unique capability is "consumer-direct fulfillment." They can ship a book in a box to anybody in the world and make it appear that it is coming from any client of theirs rather than from Ingram. So many publishers, booksellers, and other direct sellers of books use Ingram as their fulfillment capability for books ordered by consumers directly from them.

Over the past twenty years, Ingram has built a "publisher services" business through organic growth and acquisition that now make them the primary source for books from *six hundred* distinct publishers. The combined output gives them a total sales volume of a similar order of magnitude to the three smallest of the Big Five, perhaps even placing them third in a new Big Six. Ingram has built a sales organization to match, and the company is rapidly expanding other marketing services to further strengthen their clients and their distribution offer. While PRH insists on publishers of a certain size (right now that is apparently a minimum of $5 million in annual sales) for their distribution portfolio, Ingram matches Amazon. They'll take a one-book indie publisher and provide a full suite of services: printing, calling on all the bookstores, and fulfillment of print and digital content around the world.

So Ingram is positioned to keep growing as the industry changes. As Amazon attracts more and more indie authors and publishers, Ingram becomes their path to the half of the US customers Amazon might not hit and, beyond that, to the entire global marketplace. As the changes in the industry make it harder for publishers to sustain the overhead costs of warehousing, systems, and sales, Ingram provides a variable-cost alternative. And just as Amazon makes it simple and easy to reach their market with a single relationship, Ingram provides that opportunity to reach the rest of the world.

### How do these three companies relate to each other?

All these companies do business with each other. Amazon is almost certainly Penguin Random House's top account, and Ingram might be number two. Ingram sells the books of all publishers, their own distributees, and books they wholesale, to Amazon, and probably buys more books from PRH than from any other single publisher. And Amazon depends on both PRH and Ingram for the reliable supply of a big chunk of their book sales.

### What factors are already in motion that will change the publishing landscape?

There are several: books don't die anymore and disappear from the competition, and in fact, books that were thought to have died have been brought back to life in the digital no-inventory-necessary world. That adds further competition to face each new book as it is published and makes the challenge more difficult for each new commercial effort.

Bookstore and other retail shelf space is shrinking at the same time that total title output is rising.

The shift to online sales combined with the shrinking retail shelf space hurts the biggest publishers the most because their competitive advantage is largely built on their ability to put books on shelves at scale. Sales moving online could ultimately be the death knell for that competitive advantage. As things change, the winning publishers are going to be the ones who learn how to promote books so that they link directly from their online exposure to the

Amazon sales page, or those who are able to uniquely use Amazon remarketing to sell their titles.

We asked a publisher whether having one customer represent some 60 percent of all sales was more efficient, leaving time to be strategic about the remaining share. She pointed out that it was actually less efficient: just because B&N and the other accounts were selling fewer books does not mean you had to work any less hard to service them.

### How will the biggest publishers respond to the changing marketplace?

First of all, publishers will need to be acquisitive to support overheads. Their sales forces need a minimum number of books to sell to support them; their warehouses need a minimum number of books to ship to be viable. Print delivery at scale requires minimum volumes to work viably, as does store coverage. Diminishing store shelf space and reduced sales of print from press runs (as opposed to print-on-demand) will compel the big publishers to keep acquiring smaller ones for a long time. Eventually, it is likely that even the big publishers will need to combine with each other or work with Ingram to do the essential work necessary to put print books on store shelves.

Publishers will also need to change their marketing practices. They must create cheaper ways to reach consumers. That suggests both "vertical" websites, where they could get "relevant" traffic for some of their books, and "email lists." The big publishers have been collecting email "permissions" (an idea first articulated by digital thinker Seth Godin in the 1990s) for a long time. It will become increasingly important to use them well. The house with 3 million email names for a genre or a topic will have a marked advantage marketing to that audience over a publisher without such a list.

The question will be this: what does the "established" publisher have to *add* to the marketing and distribution of a title? As long as there are lots of decentralized bookstores, publishers must call on them, take orders from them, and ship to them. But as and if the ecosystem becomes more online, more e-book, and physical retail becomes more Amazon-centric, there is less and less for a publisher to contribute. Authors get much more than double the percentage of the consumer dollar through Amazon or self-publishing than they get from a publisher. If the established publisher can't expand the market, there is little incentive to sign an author and little incentive for an author to sign with them. That suggests that, over time, the movement of titles from indie success to publishers will diminish.

### Will benefits of size be replaced by, or coupled with, the ability to respond quickly to change in coming years?

While the imprint setup of the big companies has so far allowed them to react quickly, and in many cases to be responsive to a hot new acquisition that's being shown around by an agent or directly from an author in the case of a book based on breaking news, it's the larger changes that may prove a challenge. The requirement to communicate strategy, change, and corporate goals clearly and inspiringly to the staffs as large as those at the Big Five companies is not a trivial challenge, particularly in a time when uncomfortable change is often required.

Beyond communication, the publishing companies have not outlived the normal incumbent allergy to change. And so many further changes in infrastructure are needed: in manufacturing to an increasingly digital opportunistic model; in marketing and publicity and sales to gear the organization to online versus brick-and-mortar distribution that allows far less rigid title scheduling. Publishers must provide increased access to much more data—beginning with pre-publication meta-data that can be put to use in deciding where and how to spend publicity and marketing budgets up front. And then publishers need data from the field on inventory by type of account, and by region, and they need detailed point-of-sales data. Designing, structuring, gathering, storing, understanding, and then acting on all those data will require flexibility and responsiveness not usually associated with a big conglomerate.

Our experience has been that a dedicated information technology brain, not tied to the committee-driven corporate data organization, is the only way to make practical strides in this area.

### How will smaller publishers respond?

The publishing future for smaller publishers is ambiguous. On the one hand, there are services that eliminate the need for a large, expensive overhead organization. On the other hand, book sales are getting harder to make and the intermediary channel consolidating is making it harder to keep margins intact.

Smaller publishers have always tended to specialize by subject, which is an inherent advantage in the age of internet marketing. Direct consumer relationships theoretically make it possible to expand beyond books to sell other things to the same audiences. But so far, that is largely a theory. We are seeing consolidation. For example, the Anglo-American illustrated book publisher Quarto has acquired other smaller illustrated book publishers.

The shifts in retail are about twenty years old. The e-book era is about ten years old (since the Kindle). The consolidation that will tell the tale for smaller publishers is really just beginning. We'd expect many to fail and for those that succeed to have their book business be part of something larger.

### What is the future of retail?

There will always be a place for the small, specialized store that has low overhead and capitalizes on very focused curation talent. But, *if* Amazon has or develops ambitions to put more and more of their inventory into retail spaces rather than warehouses, for any other bookstores to compete with them could become very difficult. And Amazon also has the ability to create stores that aren't strictly bookstores but where books could also thrive. (Whatever they sell in the future—food or crafts or anything else—can have a "relevant books" component.) Basically, Amazon has the ability to experiment with different retail configurations more effectively and efficiently than anybody else. They've got the product *and* they have the email addresses attached to buying profiles for most of the people in the neighborhood. Every neighborhood.

### What is the future of audio?

Audio is a changed business because of digital capabilities on both the creation side and the distribution side. Creation has become a great deal simpler since most people can now record sufficient-quality audio and, through Audible, can engage any of the services they need (including somebody with a better voice than theirs) to put the production together.

But digital distribution has had the biggest impact. Before it, publishers had to get cassettes and then CDs into the hands of consumers, and the consumers had to listen while tethered to a listening device. Nowadays, everybody can download audio from the cloud to their phone. Everybody's got one. And the growth in audio reflects that.

One question for the future is whether text-to-voice (TTV) tech becomes so good that production is hardly needed at all or, even more threatening to publishers, a consumer can simply "apply" a TTV app to an e-book text and make their own audio.

We're already seeing that the combination of e-book and audio with "toggling" capability, so you can switch from reading to being read to and back, has consumer appeal. We can expect the lines to blur progressively on audio as a "separate" project in the future.

### What is the future of juvie publishing?

Juvie publishing, which comprises children's and young adult (YA), has always leaned heavily on stories and characters from outside the book world and not just from movies but also from toys. With publishing increasingly untethered from legacy publishing houses, we can expect to see the same with kids' books. In the future, almost any entity with avenues to kids—toy makers, children's clothes makers, and educational institutions among them—could "do books" as an adjunct to their existing activities. They'd do that because it isn't hard and because the kids like the "token" of a book that commemorates something else they like. Indeed, publishers have always sought licenses from kid-friendly brands. The future switch may be that those kid-friendly brands will just "do it themselves" or become partners with the publishers rather than mere licensees.

# GLOSSARY

**ABA:** American Booksellers Association, industry trade association that represents Independent Booksellers.

**advance:** has two very different uses that are ubiquitous in the book business. The "advance" is the amount the author is guaranteed by the publisher as payment for the completed book before it is published. The "advance" is also the number of copies the publisher gets orders for from accounts prior to the book's actual availability.

**agents:** specifically "literary agents" In publishing, the business representatives for authors in their dealings with publishers.

**ALA:** the American Library Association, which is the trade association for libraries; also the acronym for the two conventions held annually by the ALA.

**ARC:** "advance reading copy," usually a paperbound version of the book with a cover that isn't intended for retail. ARCs are used for pre-publication distribution of a book to get reviews or endorsements.

**audio:** short for "audiobooks," the spoken-word version of a book.

**author:** the person credited with writing a book.

**B&N:** Barnes & Noble, the largest bookstore chain in the United States.

**backlist:** the books that have been previously published by a house but are still being offered for sale; also used as a verb to describe the transition of a book to one that "sells itself" at some level following its initial publication. Big Five, or The Big Five, shorthand for the five top US trade publishing companies: Penguin Random House, HarperCollins, Hachette Book Group, Macmillan, and Simon & Schuster.

**Bertelsmann:** the German conglomerate that owns a controlling share of Penguin Random House and is still a book club power in Germany, although it no longer owns book clubs in the United States.

**blad:** a bound sample of a book, almost always an illustrated book, to show how it is designed. Blads are usually 8 to 16 pages long and attempt to show the treatment of a variety of visual elements in the book.

**boilerplate:** the standard form of a publisher's contract without any negotiated changes between publisher and author, or literary agent.

**book clubs:** formerly, primarily applied to commercial enterprises that sold books to "members" on special terms that often included some sort of automatic distribution. Now it more often refers to informal groups of readers who read the same book and then meet to discuss it.

**book contract:** the agreement between a publisher and an author by which the author assigns rights to the publisher to commercialize the work and, usually, to pay a share of revenues to the author.

**book doctors:** freelance editors hired by authors to help them recast their manuscript.

**book page:** the section of a newspaper or magazine that is dedicated to reviewing or discussing books. Often used in the negative, as in "off the book page" publicity, which means getting mention for a book in some other place in the newspaper or magazine.

**Bookscan:** the service that collects and aggregates data from cash registers to provide reporting on "actual" book sales to the industry.

**bulk:** thickness of a bound book; also a "bulking dummy," a "sample" of a book made with blank paper of the same weight and thickness that allows the publisher to get the feel of the heft of the finished book before it is printed.

**buyers:** the people in bookstores or wholesalers who make the decisions about which books to order or reorder.

**case:** the outer binding of a hardcover book. A one-piece case made of cloth used to be the norm, but it has been replaced by a one-piece paper case, or a three-piece case that uses one material for the spine and another for the rest of the binding.

**Caldecott Medal:** the award given annually by the Association for Library Service to Children, a division of the American Library Association, to the artist of the most distinguished American picture book for children published that year. The award was created in 1938.

**cast-off:** the process whereby the page count of the final book is estimated by counting characters and applying a type design to a proposed trim size.

**CBA:** the Christian Booksellers Association, the trade association of Christian bookstores.

**chain stores:** many stores that have common branding and ownership. The two big "chains" still operating in US book publishing are Barnes & Noble and Books-a-Million. The leading UK bookstore chain is Waterstone's. The leading Canadian bookstore chain is Chapters Indigo.

**composition:** the act of setting type.

**consumer dollars:** expressing sales in the dollars paid at the register by the consumer versus wholesale dollars, which are those paid to the publisher by retailers.

**consumer publishing:** the book publishing activity intended for general readers, rather than for a special professional or educational audience. Most consumer publishing is "trade," although there is still some consumer publishing activity that is "direct to consumer."

**contribution:** the dollars and cents of margin that a book generates from its sales after deduction of the direct costs of producing that single copy and paying the author.

**co-op:** the advertising that is mostly or entirely paid for by the publisher from allocations earned by the account through ordering the publisher's books.

**copyediting:** editing that both makes a book consistently conform to the house's style rules and serves as direction for composition.

**design:** the specifications for how the words and art will be placed in a book. This includes type fonts and sizes, and "treatment" of illustrations of all kinds and captions.

**digital:** most frequently these days refers to a nonprint rendition of intellectual property, but also to longtime publishing processes that were manual but have now become digital, and to the shift to digital media for marketing titles as well as to online sales of print and digital products.

**digital inkjet printing:** new method of printing books in which the unit cost does not go down by volume and that allows publishers to print closer to known demand.

**dime novels:** another name for the mass-market paperback—in this case started in the 1880s.

**discount:** the reduction from the retail price that the publisher offers an intermediary to provide margin for the supply chain.

**discounting:** the practice by stores of selling books for less than the publisher's set retail price.

**drop-ins:** titles added mid-season or outside the seasonal publishing schedule, a practice that has become increasingly common as the share of sales made through bookstores, for which the whole seasonal system was created, goes down.

**earn out:** a term that describes the point when an author's earned royalties through sales of books and rights exceed the advance paid by the publisher.

**e-book:** the digital version of a book in any nonprint format.

**embossing:** raised areas on a book jacket meant to give it a 3-D effect, or other emphasis that makes the jacket stand out.

**end-papers:** the inside front and back of a book jacket that can be left blank or printed with maps, a design, or something related to the book.

**fasicles:** parts of a serialized work.

**free sheet:** generally an acid-free paper used to make a book. Also "sheet."

**frontlist:** the titles in a publisher's catalog that are being offered for sale for the first time.

**full cloth:** see "case."

**galleys:** today, an advance copy of a book, physical or digital. The term originally referred to proofs of a book still being typeset at a time when the actual type was placed on trays called galleys before the book was "paginated" into the actual pages that would appear in the finished product.

**groundwood:** book paper that is not acid free and is likely to brown over time.

**hardcover:** a bound book with a "board" cover.

**ID distributors:** wholesalers whose origin and perhaps still principal business was delivering magazines and paperback books to accounts that were not staffed or equipped to make individual title buying decisions themselves. ID distributors have largely morphed into conventional wholesalers who sell books in response to orders from retail accounts.

**independents:** bookstores that are owner-managed and not part of a chain or other conglomerate.

**ISBN:** the International Standard Book Number, a unique number to identify a specific title in a specific format. A book's hardcover, paperback, e-book, and audio editions will all have different ISBNs.

**Kindle:** Amazon's dedicated reading device and the format of e-books it displays, often now on multifunction devices through an app.

**literary agents:** see "agents."

**managing editorial:** title not the same as with magazines. In book publishing, this refers to the largely administrative (not editorial) function of moving a book through the many stages of work that take it from manuscript to finished book.

**manufacturing:** the printing and binding process that begins after a book has been composed, designed, and made into finished pages.

**manuscript:** the book as it comes from the author.

**margin:** what remains after the cost of goods and direct operating expenses are deducted from sales.

**mass market:** uniquely in the book business, a format for paperback books that are "rack-sized." They are also known as pocket books because their dimensions—4.25" x 7"—allow them to fit in the pockets of clothing. And mass-market paperbacks were standardized to enable independent distributors to put them in standard-sized "pockets" in standardized racks placed in accounts that would usually otherwise have no way to "shelve" books.

**mass merchants:** a class of accounts in the book business that ranges from the Warehouse Clubs, to Walmart, K-Mart, and other retailers that stock a limited number of book SKUs but each in high volume. Strong sales come with a high returns rate.

**merchandisers:** staff at the chain booksellers responsible for display, special pricing, and other variables in how books are presented in the field. Cousins to "rack jobbers" who went from account to account each month, restoring order to mass-market paperback fixtures, removing old titles and replacing them with new ones.

**merchants:** staff at the chain booksellers responsible for companywide title planning, seasonal displays, and price promotions.

**metadata:** the data that describe a book. "Core metadata" are unchanging and objective: the book's trim size, number of pages, and price. Other metadata are more subjective: the book's subject matter, description of audience, endorsements, and recently the comments readers append to a title online.

**model:** in the book business, this refers to the "ideal" or "maximum" number of copies a store will stock of a book, usually within a system that automatically orders more to "top up" to the model.

**MS:** short for manuscript.

**negative option:** the direct marketing mechanism whereby the monthly selection of a book club is shipped to the consumer unless the consumer explicitly rejects it between when it is announced and when it would ship.

**Newbery Medal:** medal awarded annually by the American Library Association to the author of the most distinguished children's book published the previous year.

**Nook:** B&N's dedicated reading device.

**offset:** the printing process used most in book publishing.

**overhead:** the fixed costs required to equip a publishing house, primarily rent and staff salaries

**P&L:** profit and loss statement; usually refers to the calculation done of the economics of each book published, both prospectively (to make the acquire-or-not decision) and retrospectively (to evaluate the book's financial performance.)

**partworks:** one of the methods of selling a longer work in parts.

**permissions:** the various grants of permission to reproduce portions of copyrighted works in a new title the author or publisher obtains from the copyright holder. Conversely, those which a publisher or author, as copyright holder, grants to creators of new works.

**plant:** the fixed investment required to get a book from an author's submission of manuscript and art to a file (these days; formerly "boards" or "film") that can be printed and bound.

**Pocket Books:** originally the name of the first major US mass-market paperback publisher; has become the generic term for standard rack-sized mass-market paperback books.

**POS:** point of sale, usually referring to hard sales data about books that have been purchased by the ultimate consumer.

**PP&B:** paper, presswork, and binding, or the manufacturing process for books.

**PR:** public relations—the more formal name for publicity, which is everything from sending out press releases to all the coverage a book gets in the media.

**preorders:** traditionally the level of advance orders a publisher received from bookstore accounts for a new title. In the age of online sales, it refers to consumer orders for books before publication, with delivery on the day they are released. In addition to capturing demand early, the preorders become part of the first week sales and can put a book on the bestseller list.

**print-on-demand:** the technology that enables the delivery of a single copy of a book at a price that is usually low enough to enable a commercial transaction.

**proofs:** all or part of a book in typeset form used for checking for accuracy or for further editing.

**proposal:** the materials submitted by an author or agent to sell a project to the publisher. Often includes a table of contents, description of the market, author bio and credentials, and a sample chapter to show writing style.

**pub date:** short for publication date, which is the date set by the publisher for the official "debut" of each book. The intention is that no consumer reviews should appear before that date nor that any copies be delivered to consumers before that date. The pub date is a device intended to maximize the impact of each book's initial appearance.

**public domain:** the description of the status of a book, or any intellectual property, not protected by copyright. This can happen because the copyright term has expired or for other reasons.

**publicity:** see "PR." The coverage for a book in all forms. Also the name of the department at a publishing house charged with maximizing publicity for the list.

**publisher dollars:** sales in publisher dollars, generally net of any retail discounts.

**rack-sized:** the standard-sized mass-market paperback, 4¼" x 7", intended to fit the standard "pockets" of a display rack.

**remainder:** as a verb, the act by a publisher of selling the leftover stock from a previously issued book that has stopped selling to a broker who puts the books back into retail distribution at a sharply reduced price; as a noun, it refers to a book that is in that stage of its life.

**returns:** the copies of books that were purchased by retailers or wholesalers that are now being sent back to the publishers for credit.

**royalty:** the share of each book's revenue that is contractually promised to the author.

**sales representative, or sales rep:** person whose job is to call on bookstore, library, and, wholesale accounts to inform them and take their orders for a publisher's books; there are "freelance" or "commissioned" sales representatives who are not on salary to any house but deliver this service on behalf of many houses for a share of the sales generated.

**seasons:** in trade book publishing, refers to the grouping of titles into "seasonal lists" for the sales representatives to present to accounts. Most houses work with two or three seasonal lists per year. The recent consolidation of the business in favor of "national accounts" has changed the paradigm because those accounts are sold "monthly." Seasons are intended to enable reps to get to all their accounts once a season. In addition "drop-ins"—titles added mid-season or outside the seasonal schedule—have become common.

**self-publishing:** generally refers to authors' use of one of the tools available on Amazon or a number of other sites to post a manuscript for sale.

**serial, serialized, first serial, second serial:** words applying to the practice of publishing in pieces of a book through another publication, usually a magazine but sometimes a newspaper. Serialization can refer to one excerpt or, less frequently, more of the book published in multiple parts.

**sheet:** see "free sheet."

**SKU:** stock keeping unit, which is the specific title and edition that the store or wholesaler is tracking for sale. The number of SKUs is the number of different items available for sale.

**social media:** essentially media produced by its users, e.g., Facebook, Twitter, YouTube.

**special sales:** sales made to accounts outside the book trade. Sales to and through nonbook retailers and mail order catalogs and online sites constitute the vast bulk of special sales activity. As bookstores diminish in number, the special sales departments have become increasingly important, particularly for publishers of nonfiction books.

**subsidiary rights:** the right, normally sold by the publisher through a license, to exploit the intellectual property in a book through other forms besides the book itself being sold by the publisher. Subsidiary rights include serialization, or the right to print part of the book in a periodical or a website; paperback rights when the hardcover publisher is not the paperback publisher; book club rights; foreign rights, generally the right to reprint in translation; and audio rights when the audio is being published outside the originating publisher.

**supply chain:** literally the chain of intermediaries from the publisher to the reader and the logistics that connect them, allowing the flow of inventory and demand management necessary to feed wholesalers, bookstores, libraries, and online retailers that serve consumer demand.

**children's books:** the books, or the division of trade publishing that produces books, for children ages 1 to 16 in a variety of different formats matched to different age groups.

**TofC:** table of contents, or the listing of a book's chapters by title with reference to the page at which they begin; found at the very front of most books.

**trade discount:** the reduction from a book's publisher-set retail price that is offered to the "trade"—bookstores and wholesalers. Libraries are also part of the trade, but publishers often do not offer discounts to libraries for ordering directly from them. Most libraries source from wholesalers because these suppliers give them useful cataloging services and the libraries can order books from many publishers at the same time.

**trade paperback:** paperback books that are normally issued by trade publishers who have no particular relationships with the mass-market distribution system; these books normally have the same trim size as the prior hardcover version of the same book, if there is one, or, if an original, a trim size that approximates a normal hardcover trim size rather than the smaller "mass-market paperback" rack size.

**trade publishing:** book publishing that is aimed primarily at bookstores for distribution rather than through other channels. Professional books, academic books, and textbooks rely far less on bookstores, if they are sold through them at all, and are outside the category of "trade" publishing.

**trim size:** the dimensions—height and width—of the pages of a bound book.

**used:** books sold by their initial owner. Until Amazon, used books lived in their own network of used bookstores, only very loosely connected to each other. Since Amazon has created the ability to list used books on offer by title, it is likely (although impossible to prove or document) that most used book sales take place on the Amazon platform today. Certainly, there are far fewer used bookstores than there used to be, but there are more used booksellers given the transparency available to small, home vendors.

**work for hire:** a manuscript commissioned by a publisher for a flat fee with no ongoing royalty. The publisher owns all rights.

**young adult, or YA:** titles that are the bridge between children's publishing and adult books, aimed at readers from ages 12 to 18. Most often published as series titles, they increasingly cross over into adult readership.

# INDEX

Above the Treeline, 45
academic publishers, 4–5, 21, 92–93
acquiring editors, 17
acquisition profit and loss statement, 72–75
acquisitions, of children's books, 111–12
ACX, 124
advance orders, 28, 32, 44, 151
advance reading copy (ARC), 108, 145
advances, 21–22, 145
affiliate relationships, 89
agency pricing, 65–69, 99–100
agents
  commissions for, 14
  defined, 145
  function of, 12–15
  and subsidiary rights, 29
  tactics of, 15–16
Alfred A. Knopf Inc., 50
Amazon
  agency pricing and, 67–68, 99–100
  and business with Penguin Random House and Ingram, 138

children's books and, 110
competitiveness of, 102–3
competitors of, 91–92
early impact of, 92–93
e-books and, 60, 61, 62–65, 94–96
evolution of publishers' views of, 93–94
evolution of publishing and strategy of, 103–4
and future of retail, 142
in future trade book business, 133–34
imitation of, 90–91
influence of, 81–83, 105
initial directory of offerings by, 88
and innovations in online retailing, 89–90
and nontraditional publishing, 123–24, 132
and practical implications of mergers and consolidations, 79
quantifying growth of, in book business, 83–86
reasons for starting in book business, 11, 86–88
returns and, 35

Amazon (Cont.)
and self-publishing business,
96–98, 100–101
success of subscription
offering of, 104–5
and used book market, 98–99
Amazon Marketplace, 90,
98, 102
Amazon Prime, 90
American Booksellers
Association (ABA), 145
American Library Association
(ALA), 106, 145
Apple, 65–67, 69
ARC (advance reading copy),
108, 145
Association for Christian
Retail, 5–6
Audible, 118–19, 124, 142
audience research, 36–37, 39
audio, 145. See also audiobooks
Audio Book Creation
Exchange, 118
audiobooks
abridged, 115–16
and Amazon's e-book
business, 95
and Amazon's role
in nontraditional
publishing, 124
appeal of, 131–32
as "cheating," 117
current landscape of, 113–14
development process
for, 119–21
future of, 142–43
key players in, industry, 114
resistance to, 114–16
technology and spread
of, 117–18
and unique aspects of
Audible, 118–19
author, 145

backlist, 35, 44–45, 53, 54–55, 70,
107, 146
Baker & Taylor (B&T), 33, 88
Barnes & Noble (B&N), 31,
55, 64, 82, 91–92, 146. See
also BN.com
B. Dalton, 54–55
Bertelsmann, 92, 145
bestseller lists, 44, 105
Bezos, Jeff, 11, 82–83, 87, 88, 89
Bible publishing, 5–6
bidding, 16
Big Five, 7, 78, 123, 137, 140,
146. See also Hachette Book
Group; HarperCollins;
Macmillan; Penguin
Random House; Simon &
Schuster
blad, 146
Bloom, Harold, 116
BN.com, 60, 61, 92
boilerplate contracts, 13, 150
book clubs, 29–30, 50, 110, 129–
30, 131, 146
book contracts, 13, 17–18,
146, 150
book dimensions, 22–24
book doctors, 146
book fairs, 30, 110
book jackets, 24–25
Book-of-the-Month Club, 130
book page, 146
book popularity,
forecasting, 36–37
book printing, 26–28
book production, 25–26
book proposals, 13, 17–18
Bookscan, 85, 108, 146
Books Online, 92
Books on Tape, 114
bookstores
distribution through, 31–32
evolution of network, 53–56

in history of book trade, 50–51
how books get to, 44–46
placement in, 46–47
Book Surge, 96–97
"book trade," 2
Borders, 55, 91–92, 103
bound galleys, 40
Brilliance Audio, 114
budget. See profit and loss
(P&L) statement
bulk, 23–24, 146
buyers, 32, 41, 146

Cader, Michael, 127
Caedmon Records, 114
Caldecott Medal, 106, 147
cart marketing, 48
case, 24, 147
cast-off, 23, 147
CD-ROM, 58, 59
Cerf, Bennett, 50
chain stores, 147. See also Barnes
& Noble (B&N)
children's publishing and books
acquisition and editorial
process for, 111–12
backlist and classic titles
in, 107
consistent sales growth in, 108
defined, 154
formats of, 112
future of, 143
publicity and marketing
of, 111
sale of, 110–11
viewed as separate from adult
publishing, 106–7
versus young adult
publishing, 108–9
Christian Booksellers
Association (CBA), 5–6, 147
classic titles, 107
college textbook publishers, 4

composition, 147
consolidations, 7, 79–80, 141
consumer book publishing. See
trade book publishing
consumer-direct fulfillment, 137
consumer dollars, 140, 147
consumer publishing, 56, 147
contracts, 13, 17–18, 146, 150
contribution, 78, 147
contribution margin, 76
cookies, digital, 47–48
co-op advertising allowance,
46, 147
copyediting, 147
CreateSpace, 97, 124, 125
Crown Bookstore, 55

dated billing, 44
delivery dates, 89
department stores, 54
design, 76, 119–20, 148
Dickens, Charles, 128
digital book. See e-books
digital inkjet printing, 148
digital marketing
techniques, 47–48
digital printing, 27–28
dime novels, 130–31, 148
discount / discounting, 47, 55,
65, 66, 102, 148, 154
discovery, 40–41
distribution
of academic
publications, 4–5
avenues for, 32–34
early, of paperbacks, 52
and evolution of bookstore
network, 53–56
and future of audio, 142–43
negative option, 131, 150
preorders and, 38, 42–44
and supply chain, 44–46
through bookstores, 31–32

Donnelley, 125
Doran, George H., 50
Doubleday, 45
Doubleday, Doran, 50
Doubleday, Frank Nelson,
    Sr., 49
Doubleday & McClure, 49–50
drop-ins, 148, 153
drop-shipping, 91
Dutton, E. P., 130

earn out, 148
e-books
    acclimation to, 61
    agency model of pricing,
        65–69, 99–100
    Amazon and kick-start
        of, 94–96
    Amazon's impact on, 62–65
    and Amazon's influence on
        publishing, 81–82
    beyond Amazon, 125
    dedicated e-readers and
        multipurpose devices'
        impact on, 64–65
    defined, 148
    difficulty of predictions
        regarding, 57
    early failed attempts at, 57–59
    evolution of formats, 59–61
    and evolution of industry
        data discernment, 84–85, 86
    in history of book trade, 56
    and nontraditional
        sales, 122–23
    sales trends in
        traditional versus
        nontraditional, 127–28
    and self-publishing
        business, 100
    subscription offers for, 104–5
editing
    agents and, 14–15

of children's books, 111–12
copyediting, 147
and publication
    timeframe, 28–29
el-hi textbook publishers, 4
email lists, 139
embossing, 25, 148
end-papers, 24, 148

fascicles, 128, 148
field representatives, 32
first serial rights, 30
first-week sales, 43, 105
floppy disks, 58
foreign ownership, 9–10
foreign rights, 30
Frankfurt International Book
    Fair, 30
Frederick Stokes Company, 130
free sheet, 24, 148
frontlist, 70, 76, 148
full cloth. See case

galleys, 40, 149
genre publishing, 103–4
Grant, Ulysses S., 50
groundwood, 149

Hachette Book Group, 7, 49
Harcourt Brace
    Jovanovich, 35–36
hardcover, 22–23, 24, 149
Harper & Row, 49
HarperCollins, 7, 49, 134
history of publishing
    evolution of bookstore
        network, 53–56
    evolution of modern book
        trade, 50–51
    evolution of paperback
        industry, 52–53
    founding of major publishing
        houses, 49–50

nontraditional
   publishing, 128–29
rise of paperbacks, 51–52
house overheads, 76–78

I2S2 (Ingram Internet Support
   Services), 91
iBooks, 65–66, 69
iBookstore, 67
imprints
   and bidding process, 16
   defined, 7–8
   of Penguin Random
      House, 72
   proliferation of and
      challenges posed by, 8–9
independent (ID) wholesalers,
   3, 52, 53, 149
Independent Publishers
   Group, 32
independents, 32, 55, 118, 149
index, 29
industry data
   discernment, 83–85
Ingram Publisher Services
   Amazon and, 87, 88, 89, 91, 96
   and business with Penguin
      Random House and
      Amazon, 138
   distribution through, 32, 33
   and evolution of bookstore
      network, 55
   in future trade book business,
      133, 136–38
   internet, impact of, on
      marketing practices, 39–41.
      See also online retail
iPad, 65–66
iPhone, 64, 65
ISBN, 54, 149

jackets, 24–25
Johnson, Samuel, 106–7

Kindle, 62–64, 69, 81–82, 94–96,
   97–98, 149
Kindle Unlimited, 104–5
Kirshbaum, Larry, 103
Klopfer, Donald, 50
Knopf, Blanche and Alfred, 50
Kobo, 64
Kozol, Jonathan, 116

Lane, Allen, 51
libraries, 33
Lightning Print, 96, 125
Listening Library, 114
literary agents. See agents
Literary Guild, 50
Little Brown & Company, 49
"Look Inside" online
   feature, 93–94
Luce, Henry, 50

Macmillan, 7, 78
malls, 54
managing editorial, 149
manufacturing, 149
manufacturing costs, 26
manuscript, 13, 14–15, 20, 21,
   23–24, 28–29, 149. See also
   selling manuscripts
margins, 76, 149
marketing
   of children's and YA books,
      108, 109, 111
   internet's impact on, 39–41
   mainstream digital techniques
      in, 47–48
   and methods for reaching
      consumers, 31
   and outsourced sales, 42
   and profit and loss
      statement, 18–30
   and publication timeframe, 28
   and requirements for
      contracts, 18

marketing (Cont.)
  sales representatives' role
    in, 41–42
  and store placement, 46–47
  timing of, 38
marketing department, 37–38
Market Partners International
    (MPI), 82–83
market research, 36–37, 39
mass-market paperbacks,
    130–31, 150
mass-market
    publishing, 2–4
mass merchants, 31, 33, 150
McClure, Samuel, 49
McCormack, Tom, 78
merchandisers, 150
merchants, 150. *See also* mass
    merchants
mergers, 7, 79–80, 141
metadata, 85, 93, 150
microfiche, 55
Microsoft, 58
Mobi, 60–61
model stock, 54–55, 150
MS. *See* manuscript
MS Reader, 59–61, 63
multiple submissions, 15, 16

National Book Network, 32
negative option distribution,
    131, 150
NetGalley, 40
New American Library, 36
Newbery Medal, 106, 151
nontraditional publishing and
    sales. *See also* audiobooks;
    e-books; self-publishing
  Amazon's role in, 123–24
  beyond Amazon, 124–25
  book clubs and, 129–30
  e-book sales in traditional
    versus, 127–28

and history of
    publishing, 128–29
  impact of, 122–23, 132–33
Nook, 64, 69, 151

offset print runs, 27, 151
Onebook, 119
one-click ordering, 90
online retail. *See also*
    Amazon; BN.com
  Amazon's innovations
    to, 89–90
  children's books and, 110–11
  growth of, 2
  in history of book trade, 56
  marketing techniques in,
    39–41, 47–48
  preorders and, 43–44
  shift to, 138–39
  and used book
    market, 98–99
outsourced sales, 42
overheads, 76–78, 151
overprinting, 27
Oxford University Press, 5
Oyster, 104

Palm Pilot, 60–61, 62, 63
paper
  and printing, 26–27
  type of, 24
paperbacks, 51–53, 130–31, 154
partworks, 151
Peanut Press, 59–60
peer review, 5
Penguin, 51
Penguin Random House, 7, 27,
    42, 70–71, 133, 134–36, 138
permissions, 139, 151
*Pickwick Papers* (Dickens), 128
plant, 26, 151
pocket books, 3, 130–31
Pocket Books, 51, 151

PocketPC, 60
point-of-sale data, 54
popularity, forecasting, 36–37
POS (point-of-sale), 54, 83–84,
    141, 151
PP&B (paper, printing, and
    binding), 26, 151
PR, 151
preorders, 38, 42–44, 105, 151
price breaks, overprinting
    based on, 27
pricing. *See also* discount /
    discounting
    and Amazon's beginning in
        book business, 88
    of e-books, 65–69
printing, 26–28
print-on-demand, 91, 96–97,
    125, 136, 152
production, 25–26
production editors, 25–26
professional publishing, 4–5,
    21, 92–93
profit and loss (P&L) statement
    creation and purpose
        of, 18–19
    and decision to publish
        book, 19–20
    defined, 151
    items factored into, 20–30
    and title acquisition, 72–75
profit calculation, 75–79
promise date for delivery, 89
proofs, 25, 40, 152
proposals, 13, 17–18, 152
pub date / publication date, 32,
    42–43, 152
publication timeframe, 28–29
public domain, 152
publicity and publicity
    department, 37, 152. *See also*
    marketing
publisher dollars, 152

publisher's retail price, 20–21,
    47. *See also* discount /
    discounting
publishing business model
    construction of publishing
        companies, 72
    how trade publishers make
        money, 70–71
    implications of consolidations
        and mergers, 79–80
    math of title
        acquisition, 72–75
    profit calculation, 75–79
publishing houses
    construction and
        re-construction of, 72
    founding of major, 49–50
publishing industry. *See also*
    history of publishing;
    publishing business model
    data discernment for, 83–85
    factors influencing future
        of, 138–39
    future of retail in, 142
    future of smaller publishers
        in, 141–42
    key segments of global, 1
    publishers' response to
        changing, 139–40
    size versus speed in future
        of, 140–41
    unique aspects of, 10–11
    various segments in, 1
Pubtrack, 85

Quarto, 141

rack-sized, 3, 53, 130–31, 152
Random House, 50, 67–68
*Reader's Digest*, 50
Recorded Books, 114
religious publishing, 5–6
remainder, 152

remarketing, 47–48
Rep 2.0 program, 42
retail price, 20–21, 47. *See also*
    discount / discounting
returns, 27, 34–36, 51, 152
rights sales, 22. *See also*
    subsidiary rights
Rocketbook, 59
Roosevelt, Theodore, Jr., 49–50
royalties
    advances against, 21–22, 145
    defined, 152
    and retail price, 20
    and self-publishing business,
        100–101
    variations in rates for, 22

sales
    book jackets' impact on, 24–25
    terms of, 47
sales department, 37
sales representatives, 41–42, 153
Scholastic, 110
Schuster, M. Lincoln, 50, 51
Scribd, 104
seasons, 51, 72, 153
self-publishing, 96–98, 100–101,
    123, 124, 125, 126–27, 153
selling manuscripts
    and acquiring editor, 17
    agents role in, 12–16
    bidding in, 16
    and requirements for
        contracts, 17–18
Send-a-Book, 119
serial / serialization,
    128–29, 153
Serman, Harry, 50
Shatzkin, Leonard, 23, 45, 77–78
sheet. *See* free sheet
shopping malls, 54
Simon, Richard L., 50, 51
Simon & Schuster, 7, 50, 51

SKUs, 54, 153
smaller publishers, future
    of, 141–42
smartphones, 64
social media, 111, 153
Softbook, 59
Sony Reader, 61, 62, 63
special sales, 33–34, 45–46, 153
Spoken Arts, 114
St. Martin's, 78
Stokes, Frederick, 129–30
subscriptions, 50
subsidiary rights, 29–30, 154
success, forecasting, 36–37

tablets, 64
terms of sales, 47
textbook publishers, 4
text-to-voice (TTV) tech, 143
*Time* magazine, 50
title acquisition, 72–75
TofC, 154
trade book publishing
    components of, 2
    defined, 1–2, 155
    focus on, 6
    impact of nontraditional sales
        on, 122–23
    and mass-market
        publishing, 2–4
    organization of, 7
    revenue from, 70–71
    textbook publishing versus, 4
trade discount, 154
trade paperback, 154. *See also*
    paperbacks
trim size, 22–24, 155
trim size rationalization, 23
Twain, Mark, 50

Undercover Book Service, 90–91
unit cost accounting, 72–75
university presses, 4–5

unsold books, 27, 34–36, 51
used books, 98–99, 155

volume rights, 29

Waldenbooks, 54, 55
Warner Books, 49
wholesalers, 33
William Collins, 49
Willingham, Daniel, 117
work for hire, 52, 155

young adult publishing
  and books
  adult consumers of, 109
  versus children's
    publishing, 108–9
  defined, 155
  formats of, 112
  future of, 143
  publicity and marketing
    of, 111
  sale of, 110–11